The House of Islam

KENNETH CRAGG

Gonville and Caius College,
Cambridge, England

DICKENSON PUBLISHING COMPANY, INC.

Belmont, California

THE RELIGIOUS LIFE OF MAN
Frederick J. Streng, Series Editor

Understanding Religious Man
Frederick J. Streng

The House of Islam
Kenneth Cragg

Japanese Religion: Unity and Diversity
H. Byron Earhart

Chinese Religion: An Introduction
Laurence G. Thompson

forthcoming:

The Hindu Religious Tradition
Thomas J. Hopkins

The Buddhist Religion
Richard H. Robinson

Library of Congress Catalog Card No.: 77-76236

Printed in the United States of America

Table of Contents

Foreword

The Religious Life of Man series is intended as an introduction to a large, complex field of inquiry—man's religious experience. It seeks to present the depth and richness of religious concepts, forms of worship, spiritual practices, and social institutions found in the major religious traditions throughout the world.

As a specialist in the language and culture in which a religion is found, each author is able to illuminate the meanings of a religious perspective and practice as other human beings have experienced it. To communicate this meaning to readers who have had no special training in these cultures and religions, the authors have attempted to provide clear, nontechnical descriptions and interpretations of religious life.

Different interpretive approaches have been used, depending upon the nature of the religious data; some religious expressions, for instance, lend themselves more to developmental, others more to topical studies. But this lack of a single interpretation may itself be instructive, for the experiences and practices regarded as religious in one culture may not be the most important in another.

The Religious Life of Man is concerned with, on the one hand, the variety of religious expressions found in different traditions and, on the other, the similarities in the structures of religious life. The various forms are interpreted in terms of their cultural context and historical continuity, demonstrating both the diverse expressions and commonalities of religious traditions. Besides the single volumes on different religions, the series offers a core book on the study of religious meaning, which describes different study approaches and examines several modes and structures of religious awareness. In addition, each book presents a list of materials for further reading, including translations of religious texts and detailed examinations of specific topics.

We hope the reader will find these volumes "introductory" in the most significant sense: an introduction to a new perspective for understanding himself and others.

Frederick J. Streng
Series Editor

Preface

"France," George Bernard Shaw once observed, "is such a great country. What a pity to waste it on the French." The sentiment, of course, might equally well be set down about every land and its people. How much more, then, about religions. "Christianity is so rich a faith: what a tragedy it is held by Christians." In any study, such as this of Islam and Muslims, it is imperative to keep a balance between a true and worthy appreciation of the essential faith, and an honest open realism about its fortunes in the tumult of the world. The doctrinal and the actual, the ideal and the empirical, must always judge and address each other. To keep them in related focus is no easy task.

To attempt it, and be confined to an "introduction," is to encounter sharpened problems. There are few general statements that do not require qualification and reserve. But one cannot take in fourteen centuries with a microscope. So all that follows here is no more than an essay in interpretation. It aims to be as adequate as its limitations admit, for purposes of initial acquaintance with Islam, and in preliminary elucidation of its central themes, and for use—within these limitations—as a single text. But it will have failed if it does not leave the strong impression of the need to look further—a hope which the brief, annotated bibliography is intended to suggest and inform. The final entries there may be excused and explained, on the plea that, writing in this way about a theme which an author knows in his heart deserves so much more and better, he may be allowed to indicate what that more should be. Beyond all bibliography are the occasions of human exchange and community within and across the frontiers of faiths.

K. C.

Table of Dates

The Muslim dating A.H. (*Anno Hegirae:* "in the year of the Hijrah") begins from July 16, 622 A.D., when Muḥammad emigrated from Mecca to establish his cause in Medina. A Muslim year consists of 12 *lunar* months and each, therefore, recedes approximately 11 days each *solar* year. The Muslim calendar thus gains about three years every century on the Christian calendar. The fifteenth Hijrī century is due in 1980 A.D. 1969 A.D. is 1389 A.H.

It was considered tedious to insert both A.H. and A.D. dates in the text. The following table may assist an appreciation of chronology in relation to Islamic beginnings.

A.H.		A.D.
52 yrs. before H.	Birth of the Prophet	570
12/13 yrs. before H.	First experience of the Qur'ān	609/10
7 yrs. before H.	First Muslims find refuge in Ethiopia	615
–	The Hijrah	622
2	Muḥammad's victory at Badr	624
3	Muḥammad's reverse at Uḥud	625
8	Conquest of Mecca and the consolidation of Islam	630
11	Death of Muḥammad	632
13	Death of Abū Bakr, first Caliph	634
14/15	Capture of Damascus and Jerusalem	636
18/19	Conquest of Egypt and Persia	639/40
23	Murder of 'Umar, second Caliph	644
32	Recension of the Qur'ān	653
35	Murder of 'Uthmān, third Caliph	656
40	Assassination of 'Alī, fourth Caliph	661
41/132	The Umayyad Caliphate	661/750
61	Massacre of Karbalā' and death of Ḥusain	680
92	Muslim conquest, under Ṭāriq, crosses from Morocco into Spain	711
94	Entry into Indus Valley and capture of Multan	713
110	Death of Ḥasan al-Baṣrī, earliest Sufi	728
114	Battle of Tours: turn of the tide of Islam in France	732
132	Rise of the 'Abbāsid Caliphate	750
148	Imām of the Seveners goes into "hiddenness"	765
150	Death of Abū Ḥanīfah, great early legist	767
179	Death of Mālik ibn Anas, founder of the second School of Law	795
193	Death of Hārūn al-Rashīd of the 'Abbāsid "golden age"	809
204	Death of Abū 'Abdallāh al-Shāfi'ī, founder of the third School of Law	820
241	Death of Aḥmad ibn Ḥanbal, founder of the fourth School of Law	855
256	Death of Al-Bukhārī, great traditionalist	870
264	Imām of the Twelvers goes into "hiddenness"	878
297	Rise of the Fāṭimids in North Africa	909
324	Death of Al-Ash'arī, leading theologian	935
339	Death of Al-Fārābī, the Muslim Aristotle	950

A.H.		A.D.
345	Seljuk Turks Islamize	956
356	Fātimids in Egypt: Cairo founded	996
426	Death of Ibn Sīnā (Avicenna)	1036
492	Crusaders capture Jerusalem	1099
505	Death of Al-Ghazālī, great architect of Muslim spirituality	1111
561	Death of 'Abd al-Qādir al-Jilānī, founder of the Qādiriyyah Order	1166
564	Accession to power of Ṣalāh al-Dīn (Saladin)	1169
616/621	Mongol devastation of Transoxiana and Khurasan	1219/24
638	Death of Ibn al-'Arabī, Spanish-Arabic mystical writer	1240
657	Sack of Baghdad by the Mongols and fall of the 'Abbāsid Caliphate	1258
"	Death of Al-Shādhilī, founder of the Shādhiliyyah Order	"
659	Mamlūks halt the Mongols in Palestine	1260
672	Death of Jalāl al-Dīn Rūmī, founder of the Mawlawiyyah Order	1273
808	Death of Ibn Khaldūn, the philosopher of history and sociologist	1406
859	Ottoman Turks capture Constantinople	1453
897	Fall of Granada: end of Muslim Spain	1492
923	Sālim I conquers Egypt and carries the last titular 'Abbāsid Caliph to Istanbul	1517
926/74	Sulaymān the Magnificent, greatest of the Ottomans	1520/66
1119	Death of Aurangzib: decline of the Mughal power in India	1707
1213	Napoleon in Egypt	1798
1218	Wahhābism victorious in Mecca and Medina	1803/04
1246	French occupation of Algeria	1830
1265	Death of Muḥammad 'Alī, founder of modern Egypt	1849
1276	Death of Muḥammad al-Sunūsī, founder of the Sanūsiyyah in North Africa	1859
1286	Suez Canal completed	1869
1298	British occupation of Egypt; French occupation of Tunisia	1881
1316	Death of Sayyid Aḥmad Khān, Indian Muslim Reformer and founder of Aligarh College	1898
1323	Death of Muḥammad 'Abduh, first of the modern Arab "modernists"	1905
1342	Abolition of the Caliphate under Atatürk	1924
1357	Death of Muḥammad Iqbāl, poet and thinker	1938
1366	Creation of Pakistan	1947
1371	Egyptian Revolution under 'Abd al-Nāṣir	1952
1370 f	Emergence of new, independent states in Asian and African Islam	1950 f

Introduction

"When my mind travels to the eighty million Muslims of Indonesia, the fifty million in China, and the several other millions in Malaya, Siam and Burma, and the hundred million in Pakistan, the hundred or more in the Middle East and the forty million in Russia, as well as the other millions in the distant parts of the world, when I visualise these millions united in one faith, I have a great consciousness of the tremendous potentialities that co-operation amongst them can achieve."[1]

The figures are obviously rounded and the locations broad and incomplete. What matters is the sentiment, whether in the lowliest of those multitudes or in the exalted station of the speaker, the President of Egypt, who sets them down in his *Philosophy of the Revolution*. There is controversy even in the context. For Jamāl 'Abd al-Nāṣir (Nasser) writes *in loco* about the use of the annual pilgrimage to Mecca as a ready, and proper, occasion for political consultation among heads of state—a plan which other opinion finds quite inconsistent with the sole devotional business of the pilgrim rites and season. It is also to be noted that, for all its sincerity, his plea for Islamic solidarity ranks only third in his priorities, after the paramount claims of Arab unity and the Egyptian obligations with Africa. Arabic and the Nile, national feeling and geography, take precedence over faith and the universal.

Even so there is an emotion in the words which finds an echo through all the territories of which they speak. Not for half a century at least has Pan-Islam been a viable political program, still less a reality of power. But it is no less, for that reason, a passion and a bond, a community of experience and shared identity, extending through a segment of the human family large enough to constitute at least one seventh of mankind.

The aim of the chapters that follow is to study the religious life of this great *Dar al-Islam*—the name, meaning "House of Islam," current among Muslims from a very early date to describe themselves. By any Muslim measure, of course, the isolation of religious life is uncongenial. For Islam, by its own showing, is a unity in which culture, society, and the political realm, no less than devotion and cultic forms, partake. It is, for Muslims, a western and deplorable notion that sees religion as separable from the totality of the human context. All must be claimed for the sacred loyalty. But, even so, it needs the ritual focus and the dogmatic structure, and these, with their kindred elements of social feeling and allegiance, may readily be permitted to do duty here for the larger whole.

The *Dār,* simply understood, is the place where things circulate in their own habitat, the abode of persons moving where they belong. The term is much more than geographical, though *Dār al-Islām* takes in every continent. There are Muslims in the Americas, as well as in Asia where they originate, and in Africa and Europe where they conquered and increased. In and beyond the territorial meaning of the phrase there belongs a whole sociological and cultural complex, with a bewildering variety of form and temper, yet all somehow self-aware and participant in one identity. The concept is often defined by reference to its antonym, *Dār al-Ḥarb,* "the House of non-Islam," "the unpeaced abode," which in the days of *Jihād,* or so-called "holy war," was yet to be brought into conformity and concord with Islam. In its old rigorous sense the distinction between Islam and non-Islam no longer holds. Face to face with secular pressures and modern conditions the two *Dārs* might be said to co-exist within every Muslim community and within every Muslim struggling for a worthy discipline of his duties and desires. No simple division of humanity into two camps, with a militancy poised and pledged to subdue the enemies of truth across a single delineated boundary, whether of map, creed, or code, any longer possesses either exterior occasion or interior validity.

While the sense of mission persists, as the obligation inherent in being Muslim, the old caliphal unity of *Dār al-Islām* has ceased this last half century. There seems no prospect of its renewal. The Arab revolt against the Ottoman Caliphate in the First World War was a remarkable assertion of the principle of nationalism at the price of Muslim against Muslim, though it is true that the excesses of the Caliphate itself in its nineteenth century Ottoman shape had themselves provoked that cleavage within collective Islam. After the war the Turks themselves took up the same principle; they vigorously abandoned their empire and the Caliphate, and moved under Atatürk's leadership into a militantly laïc, secular state, in which Islam itself was deprived. This was indeed a rare venture for Muslims, even though the sequel has demonstrated that history must see this assertion of Turkism, subduing religion to a merely sociological function, as nevertheless an event *within* Islam.

Freed from the Turks, the Arabs found themselves delayed and frustrated by continuing western imperialism in the form of mandates and by the oddly parallel, but deeply provocative, principle of Zionism, with its pursuit of statehood for Jewry. That tragedy apart, Arab nationalism is everywhere outwardly accomplished throughout the Middle East and North Africa—but accomplished in the form of fragmented territories whose boundaries, though hard to merge, represent more the competitions within the departed imperialisms than the realities of the Arab spirit. "Our frontiers," said Shukrī al-Quwaitlī, once President of Syria, "are not our limits but our wounds."

In further Asia the same problem obtains, for vastly more numerous populations. Islam in the Indian subcontinent is sundered into two political territories by the partition that gave being to the state of Pakistan. There is Islamic statehood for the majority people in the territorial concentration of their majority, but only at the cost of separating them from their own religious kindred who must subsist without it as minority people in the areas of their numerical inferiority. This is seen as the necessary consequence of statehood and as a valid price for the preservation and expression of Islam, as conceived by Pakistan. The paradox is that it entails a situation beyond its frontiers in which some fifty million Muslims in (political) India must necessarily exist, without statehood of their own, in a multireligious society where they will never predominate. This is the very fate—or vocation (depending on how you take it)—which Pakistan was conceived to deny and created to avoid. The problem is in fact more severe for India's Muslims, by the existence of Pakistan, than it would have been for the Muslims of the whole subcontinent in a conceivable all-India federal unity. This does not, however, disqualify Pakistan, either in fact or theory. It merely measures the complexity of the issues provoking Islamic nationalism and the consequences of its pursuit. Certainly the Muslims of India, on their side of the partition, have a destiny quite novel, in its dimensions and character, in the whole history of Islam: that of existing "just as a religion" without benefit of political hegemony—a condition so far from ever being congenial or normal that the phrase itself has no acceptance. Soviet Muslims share this circumstance, but in sharply special form.

Though everywhere fragmented into nations, the house of Islam is, by the same token, alive and alert. Imperialism has a deadening effect upon the inward ideology of peoples. By contrast, counterimperialism means a great stimulus to self-sufficiency in every sphere, a recovery, even if sometimes oversanguine, of the inner dynamic of religion. The resulting sense of competence gives a lively incentive to the tasks of apologists, to the theorists, evangelists and counsellors of the faith with which nationalism is allied. The stimulus is mutual; there are at once new opportunities and new occasions and, with them, new aspirations and energies. The Islam we have to study here is no subject for a misanthrope. It can only be known by a willingness to move with the pace and the ambition of its own temper.

The irony is that there is also a pace in contemporary affairs, which sorely taxes the resources of the religious will and the traditional dogma. New nationalisms have come to their own concurrently with the burgeoning populations, industrial pressures, economic disequilibrium of nations, rapid urbanization and other chronic stresses of the day. There is disenchantment as well as exuberance. The intractability of many problems of nationhood, and the sense that solutions which are vital turn on factors that are beyond local control make for a hope/despair and a love/hate relationship vis-à-vis technology and all its ways. Under these burdens it is natural that the house of Islam presents to the observer a whole variety of attitudes and a diverse chorus of voices, conserving, defending, reforming, advising, disputing, and commending, as interpretations allow and tensions dictate. Our main business with them all, aside from a lively feeling for the struggles and the strains, is to understand religious meaning. It is to see

Islam "housing" Muslims, in experience under God, as heirs to a long past of monotheistic assurance and a singularly inclusive, emphatic system of religious allegiance and observance.

What does it mean to be a Muslim today? What did it mean to be one in the first days of the Qur'ān and the immediate "companionship" (to use a technical word) of Muḥammad? What did it mean in the succeeding centuries of traditional identity and institutional continuity? Why are there Sunnis and Shī'ahs as abiding segments within the one house? Who are the Sufis, the mystics, and what was the secret of their origin and of their persistent role in Islam? And, within all these enquiries, the question: Who is the Muslim?

"Whatever the disciple is destined to discover in the Law was given to Moses on Sinai," says a tradition of Judaism. It seems almost to validate anything, until we notice the safeguard in the word "disciple." The conservative, who will fear the dictum for its threatening liberties, can still, for his comfort, disqualify from "discipleship" the interpreter of whom he disapproves. But, in the end, Sinai is what Sinai means to those who belong at Sinai. The collective is the clue to the identity that makes it. From this circularity there is no escape. There has to be a parallel saying for Islam, though it is not traditional. "Islam is what Muslims hold it to be." But they are Muslims because Islam holds them, and there will be continuing debate among them about who, and how, they properly are.

The chapters that follow are concerned with both sides of this equation—with the Islam of Muslims and with Muslims in their Islam. We proceed to it by first pondering the Lordship of God, the primal reality and the source of all else. From the transcendent rule of God all else follows—Muḥammad, the Qur'ān, Law, Liturgy and *Ummah,* the Prophet, the Scripture, the *Sharī'ah,* the rites of *Dīn* and the fact of the community or "household." After studying all these in their interrelation, this work, in the final chapter, turns to glance at what the will to fulfill itself universally has meant in the continuity of Islam.

1.

"Lord of the Worlds"

To enter into Islam it is better to go to the mosque than to reach for the dictionary. But where there is no physical opportunity for the one, we must begin from the admitted inadequacy of the other. If it is alert enough, the effort after definition can serve our ends well. Encyclopedias, it is true, all too readily turn the mystery and livingness of things into terms and technicalities, and this destroys them. Truly to know the Muslim in his faith we must somehow linger in the precincts of his prayer, kindle to the accents of the Qur'ān reciter, and feel the pulse of the fast of Ramaḍān. But, outsiders as we are, we need for these interior ventures the discipline of academic statement. Sympathy and scholarship must excite and complete each other. Only by their partnership are religions understood. The hope in these chapters is to seek and to sense the poetry of Islamic religion through the prose of Muslim doctrine, law, and community.

The great Arab-born monotheism of Asia and Africa is unique among faiths in being denoted by a term that is also a common noun. Hinduism takes its name from a land and a river, Buddhism from the meaning of a founder figure, Judaism from a people, Christianity from the concept and achievement of "the Messiah." Islam, which is never properly called "Muhammadanism," differs from all these. The name "Islam" could just as well be *islām*.[1] The Arabic language has no capital letters and, therefore, no means of indicating the significant distinction between proper names and common nouns. It uses one term inclusively for both the simple action and the historical incorporation. The distinction between *islām* and Islam may be seen as comparable to such familiar usages as labor and Labor or public health and Public Health. There is the general and the specific; there is the idea and its definitive expression, the thing in itself and the thing in its "institution." Islam organizes *islām,* enshrines and defines it. It makes Muslims of *muslims*. The active noun—what Arabic grammar calls "the name of the doer"—has the same double quality as the verbal noun. Islam is the thing and Muslims are the doers, both from a single root. Abraham, for example, was a *muslim* centuries before the Prophet Muḥammad and the Scripture, or Qur'ān, that inaugurates Muslims as history finally knows them.

This situation needs to be kept steadily in view. The faith that stems from seventh century Arabia believes itself to be continuous with all true religion and to perfect what right worship everywhere intends. It gives final, institutional form to the proper religious temper of mankind. It is the dimension by which all other relationships are to be subdued. It is ultimate religion in unambiguous definition and in true balance. The role of Islam in relation to all other faiths is to prune, correct, purge, and complete them. In the finality of the Qur'ān, God's worshipfulness and man's worship come into authentic and ultimate relation.

The fact of God, One, All-Powerful, Sovereign, Eternal, "the Lord of the worlds," is the all-embracing reality. Islam means the steady duty of the God-ward reckoning, the habit of obligation under God as the central and inclusive meaning of existence. Man in Islam is firmly and vigilantly set in the Divine milieu, not by election in distinction from others, but by dint of natural human worth, universally shared, born under the Divine mercy, destined for immortality and judgment, and meanwhile guided, exhorted, habituated, and disciplined by Islam into that conformity with the will of God which is the whole *raison d'être* of humanity.

The documentation of this theology is the Qur'ān (Koran). The means to its enunciation in the world is Muḥammad. The shape of its reception is the sacred law. The pattern of the human response is in the ritual and social duties of the faithful. By these, *islām* becomes Islam. Each of them calls for detailed exposition in the chapters that follow. But the prior duty is with the Divine. We elude the whole nature of Islamic faith if we propose to give it time or attention because we are interested in orientalism, or archaeology, or psychology, or comparison of creeds. God, by Muslim criteria of worship, cannot be the end of an argument, nor an object of discourse. The notion that other peoples' religions may be "interesting" is not the temper likeliest to do justice to the inner meaning of Muslim prostration in prayer.

But if, with this in mind, we begin with "the Lord of the worlds," the reader who is first concerned with the instrumental things may well go at once to the succeeding chapters. What they take up is here presupposed.

Ashhadu inna lā ilāha illā-llāh: Muḥammadun rasūl Allāh—such is the Islamic creed, or *Shahādah,* sometimes also called the *Kalimah,* the word that witnesses to the sole reality of God and the apostolate of Muḥammad on behalf of God. "There is no god but God and Muḥammad is the apostle of God," to which each believer prefaces the word: "I bear witness that . . ." It begins with the absolute negation of the pseudo-deities. The great struggle of the Prophet was against idolatry and tribal superstition, against belief in a variety of pagan powers thought to dwell in wells and winds and hills. His mission was to give the lie to these fictions and fears by proclaiming against them the indubitable Lordship of God. It was not that the Divine sovereignty needed this defense. It was the misguided and perverse distortions of men that required its reiteration. It is only as notions that idols need to be denied, for they have no other existence.

So "there is none but He." The word *Allāh* is incapable of a plural. There is no reluctance to pronounce its fluent syllables, such as Judaism feels over pronouncing *Yahweh*. On the contrary: let those flowing "l"s of the *Shahādah* be perpetually heard. For the very mention of God is beneficent, protective, and devout. This is the most repeated word in Muslim vocabulary, whether it be to greet a friend or to comprehend the universe. There is none save *Allāh,* whether we acknowledge a salutation or invoke the heavens. The grammarians suggest at least a score of derivations for the word. But their ingenuity is dubious. It suffices that God *is,* uniquely, unassailably, overwhelmingly. As the Hebrew New Year liturgy has it:

> God high exalted, Dynast of endlessness,
> Timeless transcendency
> Worshipped eternally,
> Lord of infinity.

Islam stands squarely in the Judeo-Christian tradition of insistent and urgent monotheism and does so all the more vehemently for its desperate polytheistic environment in pre-Islamic Arabia and the sharp, strenuous iconoclasm for which, and as which, it was born.

That original alertness against all false theologies accompanies the whole elaboration of Muslim religion. It is, as it were, a supreme "protestantism" in its very genesis, a cry of heart and a mission of will against all that violated the Divine unity or distracted men from the single direction of their love, their loyalty, and their obedience. Hence the ringing shout of praise that echoes through all Islamic ritual and dogma: *Allāhu akbar,* "Greater is God," which, grammatically, is a comparative form made all the more striking by its refusal, indeed its inability, to enter any stated comparison. "God is greater" than all that could conceivably be set in any clause after "than." The idea of framing such a clause is itself unthinkable. Yet the superlative ("God is the greatest") is not preferred, for this could imply approximate equality and would, as such, be open to ambiguity, as the psalm is which declares: "He is a great king above all gods." Are we to understand that the gods exist, if only as underlings? Or do we mean that the Lord reigns in utter majesty alone? Islam has no truck with such double possibility of intention. It was not the existence of *Allāh* that Muḥammad proclaimed. The tribes knew Him by His Name. It was His *sole* existence, negating all pluralism. God is, exalted above all that might—though always impossibly—compare with Him.

The crowning purpose of the Quranic affirmation of God is worship and submissiveness. Though capable of meticulous argumentation and sometimes busy with scholastic subtleties, Islamic dogma is essentially the handmaid of religious duty and not a pursuit in its own right. It is theology in the imperative, with the accent on law, rather than on ontology, on the will of God rather than on His being. Its genius has always been in the realm of response to the Divine claim rather than with disquisition into the Divine character. It has an instinctive sympathy with the rabbinic tradition that has God saying: "Would that they left Me alone and did My Torah." There is no merit in excessive curiosity. Direction is more important than conjecture. Religion has to do with action rather than analysis. *Ḥasbunā Allāh* runs a frequent Quranic phrase: "God is our enough." Though it may be invoked for the mystic's "unfathomable mystery," for the average Muslim it means rather that the end of all debate is the reality of the Divine, that God suffices, both for present life and future destiny, both for fidelity and for faith. It is characteristic of Islamic thought and Muslim habit to terminate, if not to foreshorten, all enquiry with the words: "God knows."

And we know all that is religiously necessary to know about God by revelation. Islam might be described as the practice of unreserving reserve. There is a reverence which draws back from the mystery of God, for there is a mastery about all knowledge which can never be proper for men in respect of God. But this "reserve" about the veiled wonder and otherness of God is, by that quality, all the more total and entire in its surrender. Islam sees itself more authentic as religion, by the very diffidence of its theology.

This situation is well illustrated in the Ninety-nine Names of God, which figure so prominently in Muslim doctrine and devotion. These *Asmā' al-Ḥusnā,* "the Excellent Names" of God, are so numbered symbolically, the hundredth Name being hidden. With a rosary, or string of beads, the worshipper tells the Divine titles as he runs the beads through his fingers. In tradition well over five hundred Names have been current. Some seventy are Quranic. Many are near duplicates of each other, being alternative derivatives from a smaller number of root verbs or concepts. Some are active participles, referring to creation, sustenance, providence, direction, and decree. Others are adjectival. It is with the latter that the significant theological tensions arise. Some short account of these may serve to underline the quality of Islamic divinity.

Adjectives, of course, take their significance in human speech from human situations. It is from human reference that they derive their content. Only so are language and literature possible, only so is it feasible to pray, to theologize, or even to speak of God at all. Yet to apply human descriptives, relevantly, to God seemed to involve religion in a situation where the Divine was being made to participate in the human, the eternal to be characterized by the temporal. This, for Muslim instinct, was intolerable, since God is wholly other than man. The Divine majesty is immune from such "identifiability" in terms of the human. "God," as John Donne used to say, "is only and Divinely like Himself."

Yet prayer, not to speak of theology, requires, and requires urgently, that we be able to say what He is "like." If, out of fear of demeaning the Divine otherness, we veto all theological description and opt for utter silence, we also silence worship. This some mystics and negative theologians may be ready to allow. But it does not do for common men. Theological silence equals religious futility. A God we cannot "name" is a God we cannot acknowledge. We cannot pray unless, in measure, we can conceive. All address is description. The Arabic verb here, *dā'a,* like the English "to call" has a double sense which enshrines the whole problem. It means to name and so to invoke, to identify and so to summon, to call and to call upon. Authentic prayer means feasible theology, even though we may readily concede that beyond both, worship goes out into mystery.

This is, plainly, the familiar theme of "anthropomorphism," or speaking of God in human categories. It applies also to phrases such as "the face of God," "the hand of God," "the arm of the Lord," as well as to adjectival Names. The issue is familiar in many creeds. But nowhere has the paradox been so uncongenial as for Islam. Nowhere has there been a greater reluctance to concede relationality toward man on the part of God, lest this should endanger the sovereignty of God and somehow open the way again for the renewal of idolatry. The classical theologians have remained loyal to the anti-idolatrous urgency of the historic genesis of their Islam. In the other monotheisms, especially in Christianity, there is a much more relaxed dogmatism of unity, no less uncompromising, but readier for "the Word" in relation with the "flesh."

Islamic reluctance here does not, of course, mean that *Allāh* is not involved with men. On the contrary, the Divine giving of the law means that there is no Divine indifference to the world. No lawgiver can be immune from concern about the reception of His commands. By enjoining *islām* and expecting it from men God stakes something of Himself on their response. If deafness or rebellion are a matter of indifference, then there is a fundamental unreality, either in the commands themselves, or in the option they summon. Such an unreality would make nonsense of the legislative will and vacuity of the Divine reign. Through law unto *islām,* God in Islam is crucially involved in human situations.

Nevertheless, to return to the Excellent Names, there is a rooted, and honorable, uneasiness for Islam about all such thoughts. Muslims prefer to believe that God's Lordship is beyond all human damage, indeed, beyond all human import. Whatever damnation they may mean for man, broken law and flouted sovereignty are somehow unharming to God. The Divine inviolability abides. All the more, then, those other involvements of the Divine with the human, namely the terms of invocation, are also outside His inaccessible character. They can still, however, be used. For they are religiously indispensable, despite their theological untenability.

This conclusion was the consensus of traditional theology in the tenth and eleventh centuries, after prolonged controversy. It was embodied in the neat formulas *bilā ḳaif* and *bilā tashbīh.* The worshipper uses the Names of God "without implying 'how' " and "without representational intention." Sovereignty and sublimity are conserved by these conclusions, at the price of imaginative warmth and confidence. Islam considers that deference here is a truer theological virtue than assurance. This theme is the Islamic form of a recurrent perplexity and tension about all religion and belongs with a large contemporary discussion on the feasibility of religious language.

Understanding this large reservation in its true temper, we have to ask, briefly, about the Names themselves. The most notable are the two that stand in the *Bismillāh,* or invocation, at the head of every Quranic chapter (except the ninth): *al-Raḥmān al-Raḥīm.* "The merciful Lord of mercy" seems the best translation, though "the compassionate, the merciful" is more familiar. The root word in both words is the same, and it seems odd to translate it with two different English terms. The difference in sense between them is progressive, moving from "mercy" as an essential quality, to "mercy" in actual bestowal. What God is, to use an old fashioned word, in "His property," He is also in His activity. In both senses, He is benign, beneficent, good, forgiving, compassionate.

Classifiers have tried to arrange the whole sequence of Names, according to frequency, emphases, affinity and context. Within the intellectual reticence already noted, they give religious confession to the sense of Divine authority, power, eternity, majesty, omniscience, decisiveness, tremendousness, and kindly forbearance. They are Names, not treatises. Their meaning withdraws into their Lord, Who wills to be so celebrated. In the words of Surah 7:180: "To God belong the Excellent Names, so call upon Him by them."

There is one dominant phrase in this theme which stands as the head of this chapter, namely *Rabb-al-ʿĀlamīn,* "the Lord of the worlds," and which opens up other vistas of our duty with the Islamic sense of God. The term *Rabb* responds to *ʿabd,* which is the most characteristic descriptive of man. He is "servant" to his "Master," God. God is the Lord of all spheres and realms. The word *Rabb,* as some modern commentators are eager to claim, may have connotations belonging to "nurture" as well as to "rule." On that ground it has been fitted into an evolutionary understanding of the world, within a loyal theism. God, so to speak, presides over all the processes and developments by which things are, and by which they move. The plural "worlds" here fits the same idea of diversity and interdependence belonging to the universe as science knows it. All that is, from planets to atoms, from the infinities of space to the intimacies of the soul, derives from the creative *fiat* of God, Who originates and undergirds them all. The word *ʿālamīn* belongs with a root having the sense of "to know." The clear implication is that the physical and material and sentient worlds are means whereby the creating power of God may be traced and discerned.

Our earlier insistence on the impenetrable transcendence of God and the Islamic reliance on revelation, not reason, as the foundation of faith, does not imply any reluctance to esteem reason in the mundane sphere. On the contrary, Islam encourages empirical observation and scientific intelligence. It argues these from the recurrent Quranic exhortation to note with gratitude and attentiveness "the signs of God" in the natural order. These are everywhere present in the open countenance of nature, where they are amenable to human interrogation and provoke to rational investigation as well as religious wonder. It is the Creator in Himself, not in His works, to Whom we have no rational access, and where even revelation brings only intimations of guidance for our actions, not of disclosure for our curiosity.

This "scientific" access to the nature of the worlds is implicit in calling them *'ālamīn*. God's presiding and ordering Lordship comprehends all that men do in culture and civilization, the whole drama of their history on the stage of nature. Man under that Lordship is a servant with a tributary authority of his own. This indeed provides the substance of his *islām*. For if he had nothing about which to be obedient, there could be no point in his obligation. Thus the Divine rule presupposes man's dignity. It is on both counts that it denies and vetoes the nature-gods and the pseudo-deities, which tyrannize over men in their ignorance and pretend against God.

Divine Lordship over the worlds is sometimes interpreted so as to make the whole of nature, as well as humanity, in some sense *muslim*. There is the concept of a natural, cosmic *islām,* in which stars and molecules, species and elements, plants and creatures, all "worship" by their very conformity to the laws of their being. This *islām* has to be understood as involving many diversities, the inert and the mobile, the material and the animal, the mineral and the living. Surah 3:83 is sometimes quoted in this connection. "Freely or otherwise, the denizens of the heavens and of the earth submit to Him." The "unwilled" submission here may well refer, however, not to inanimate nature but to obstinate humanity. In that case the passage would have to do with persons only. But whatever may be true of the rest of creation, man's is certainly the arena of the Divine will, of volitional surrender to the one Lordship. Only man is capable of this ultimate *islām* of mind and soul, and only he, by the same token, is possessed of the option of defiance.

Yet that very option is also the crux of man's high calling, his responsible creaturehood. That God is, over man, and that man is, under God, is a belief that dignifies the human dimension in safeguarding the Divine worth. The command of God hallows and exalts man as hearer and doer. His submission is his liberation. His status is realised in being religiously accepted. Islam means that man is invited to will his true being by heeding the Divine will as that which conditions and describes it.

The human calling turns on the dethroning and disowning of the false gods. "There is none save He." Men are enslaved, degraded, undone, defiled, and damned by their false worships. *Islām* does not truly happen except before the worthy God. *"Shirk"* says the Qur'ān, using two of its profoundest terms, "is great *Ẓulm*" (Surah 31:13). *Shirk* is this allowance of other gods beside God, this chronic idolatry, which denies to God alone the worship, trust, honor, and gratitude, due to Him. Such denial, precisely, is *Ẓulm,* wrong in its utmost form, the refusal of the truth of things. It is *Ẓulm* against God. But it is also *Ẓulm* against man, against ourselves. The idolater is his own worst enemy, in that he corrupts and distorts his own being in the untruth of his gods. The right surrender emancipates from the pride of evil.

One of the most familiar themes of the Divine Lordship is that which relates to human destiny in time and history. It is a common view that Muslims are traditionally "fatalistic," because of the strong emphasis of their doctrine on the power and unquestioned will of God. The opinion could be substantiated from much in Muslim attitudes, as popularly held, and also from classical Islamic theology. But western critics have often misconstrued the matter. The sense of God over all, omniscient, omnicompetent, and omnipotent, certainly dominates, even oppressively, in orthodox thinking and assumption. Some have readily identified history with God's will, in an iron grip of celestial necessity, inflexible and inescapable, to the point of denying to natural and historical causation any genuine place. All is seen, without mediating causes, as God's decree and God's deed. When puzzled about the moral accountability of men, if God is the sole author of all their deeds, the theologians found refuge in a verbal solution, by which God willed the deed *in* the will of the doer. This was held to make the action at once reprehensible and responsible, inescapable and yet accountable.

Al-Ash'arī (d. 935 A.D.), the most famous of the authors of *Kalām,* or scholastic theology, set the matter down as adamantly as any in his refutation of the *Qadariyyah* and the *Mu'tazilah,* the contemporary "freethinkers" and "libertarians." Asked about *kasb,* or "acquisition" (this doctrine that the doer "acquires" it, in his history, from God's willing it *in* him), he replied:

> It has no agent, who makes it as it really is, save God, and no one with power over it so that it will be as it really is, in the sense that he creates it, save God.[2]

In a further passage, the same author goes on to state the untrammelled will of God in terms that capture with typical blandness this aspect of Islamic faith.

> The proof that God is free to do whatever He does is that He is the supreme Lord, subject to no one, with no superior over Him who can permit, command, chide, forbid, or prescribe what He shall do and fix bounds for Him. This being so, nothing can be evil on the part of God. For a thing is evil on our part only because we transgress the limit and bound set for us and do what we have no right to do. But since the Creator is subject to no one and bound by no command, nothing can be evil on His part.[3]

All such thinkers were loathe to think their way beyond this impasse by a sense of there being a law within the Divine nature. For this, somehow, seemed disloyal to His unconditionedness.

These attitudes, however, need to be set in somewhat different focus by reference to the Qur'ān itself. It is easy enough to substantiate from it a total Divine predestination. But there are some passages clearly pointing in the other direction. There is the reiterated cry (more than a hundred times): "Perhaps ye (or they) may . . . ," linked with all the major themes of human decision—faith, perception, gratitude, and submission, and seeming to set them squarely within the province of personal will. True, there are other contexts which place belief and unbelief, goodness and evil-doing, heaven and hell, all irresistibly within the Divine dictation and irreversible decree or *qadar*. But "the grand perhaps," to borrow Browning's line, is still a deep element in the Quranic picture and, in a sense, it takes a free man to be a Muslim. For if his *islām* is utterly arbitrary, it is to that extent either meaningless or unnecessary. Self-help is certainly commended to believers. As we shall see in Chapter 2, "providence" in the early story of Islam is far from being something to wait for in passivity. Muḥammad gave robust evidence of the legitimacy and effectiveness of personal resourcefulness. There is the oft-quoted comment of Surah 13:12 that "God does not change a people's state until they change their own hearts' thoughts." The force of this, however, is blunted, though not belied, by the succeeding words: "Whensoever God desires evil for a people, there is no averting it." While it is true that there is nothing which would not have been different had God willed it otherwise, the conviction (Surah 13:18) that God is the creator of everything need not be taken in a crudely fatalistic sense.

The wisest course in this vexed theme of Islamic doctrine is not blindly to insist on the centuries old traditions of determinism, whether theoretical or popular, nor yet to fall uncritically for the free dynamism of such modern interpreters as Muḥammad Iqbāl (d. 1938 A.D.) who taught that God Himself awaited the "ego" of the human genius. Both of these incur different liabilities with the Qur'ān. It lies rather in seeing the Islamic view of events and wills as enveloped, positively, in this totality of the Divine rule. All things are to be related directly and, as it were, jealously, to the will of God. But such a zeal that no other than He be accredited the determinator did not, in Islam's genesis, and does not now preclude the vigorous role of human action.

When Islamic understanding of the Lordship of the worlds turned from these more concrete issues of destiny and will, of faith and works, to the still more metaphysical problems of the Divine unity or the status of the Qur'ān as the Divine word, it was even more inclined to leave the basic questions to silence, or to formulate the problems themselves into dogmatic "answers." This is not to say that Islamic history lacks profound philosophical curiosity and speculation. There were thinkers of the stamp of Al-Fārābī (d. 950 A.D.) and Ibn Sīnā (d. 1037 A.D.), who rank with the greatest in the western medieval world, and ambitious mystical systems with their complex formulations of Divine knowledge. Islam expanded into a world of Christian theological intellectualism and Greek rational heritage. It could hardly escape, in its first centuries, the onus of these relationships, their habits of disquisition and reflection. It shares with the west in an ancestry that includes Aristotle as well as Abraham.

There were, moreover, many implicit questions deferred, of necessity, to later times, in the initial fervor and urgency of the Islamic task under Muḥammad. These came into their own in the succeeding centuries—questions about the eternity of the Qur'ān, the role of reason in revelation, the mystery of the Divine attributes, the ontological status of prophethood, and the like. The broad consensus of the centuries, after unhappy ventures into lively controversy, was that authoritarian dogmatism was the proper posture. One of its most typical representatives was the theologian Al-Nasafī, author of *'Aqā'id,* (d. 1142), a treatise on the dogma of Islam, part of which runs as follows:

> God Most High, the One, the Eternal, the Decreeing, the Knowing, the Seeing, the Hearing, the Willing: He is not an attribute, nor a body, nor an essence, nor a thing formed, nor a thing bounded, nor a thing numbered, nor a thing divided, nor a thing compounded, nor a thing limited. He is not described by *māhiya* [what-ness], nor by *ḳaifiyyah* [how-ness], and He does not exist in place or time. There is nothing that resembles Him . . . He has qualities from all eternity existing in His essence. They are not He nor are they other than He . . . [His] Word is a quality from all eternity, not belonging to the genus of sounds and letters, a quality that is incompatible with coming to silence.[4]

In similar vein was the commentary on the first half of the *Shahādah,* contained in Al-Ghazālī's celebrated *magnum opus, The Renewal of the Sciences of Religion,* Book 2, in a series of paragraphs intended for memorizing by children.

> He in His essence is one without any partner, Single without any similar, Eternal without any opposite, Separate without any like. He is One: Prior with nothing before Him, from eternity, without any beginning, abiding in existence with none after Him, to eternity without an end, subsisting without ending, abiding without termination. . . . Measure does not bind Him and boundaries do not contain Him.[5]

On the vexed and much debated question of God's seatedness on the Throne, Al-Ghazālī wrote:

> He is seated firmly on His Throne after the manner which He has said and in the sense in which He willed a being seated firmly, which is far removed from contact and fixity of location and being established and being enveloped and being removed. The Throne does not carry Him but the Throne and those that carry it are carried by the grace of His power and mastered by His grasp. He is above the Throne and the heavens and above everything unto the limit of the Pleiades with an aboveness that does not bring Him nearer to the Throne and the heavens, just as it does not make Him further from the earth and the Pleiades . . .[6]

In each of the other themes of traditional dogma, omniscience, determining, unconditionality, Al-Ghazālī's "instructor" is equally scholastic, erudite, guarded, and prone to careful negation as a means of at once defining God and reserving Him from definition.

> Events have no place in Him and mishaps do not befall Him. He does not cease, through His various epithets, to be far removed from changing and through His perfect qualities to be independent of perfecting . . . He knows the creeping of a black ant upon the rough rock in the dark night . . . What He wills is, and what He wills not is not . . . There is no analogy between His justice and

> the justice of creatures, since tyranny is inconceivable in the case of God, though conceivable in the case of a creature dealing with property of some other than himself. He never encounters any rights in another beside Himself so that His dealing with it might be a doing of any wrong . . . No particular action toward any one is incumbent upon Him . . . and no one possesses any right against Him.[7]

The length of these extracts is justified by the cumulative effect of their insistent exoneration of the Divine, their instinct to eliminate the relationality of God and man except in the most arbitrary terms. Al-Ghazālī, and those whose orthodoxy he did so much to solidify and establish by dint of his profound intelligence and his immense prestige, embody the gathered verdict of the Islamic mind about the reality of God.

Despite its uncompromising severity, however, it is throughout an understanding about mercy and compassion. Somehow these elements were less exposed to the issues which needed such vigilance from the theologians in respect of sovereignty and will. As befits its emphasis the classic theology of Islam is less concerned about the "comfort" of man than it is about the majesty and immunity of God, since these must be seen as, in every event, a prerequisite of the mercy. In its own urgent way, the Qur'ān is warmer, kindlier, more compassionate than the theologians. While the Book of Islam underwrites and prompts the latter in many of their concerns and something of their temper, its vitality and fervor, its mission and movement, bring the reader into a different world from the aridity and calculation of the dogmatists.

There remain, in general terms, three fundamental questions belonging to the Islamic sense of God. They have to do with superstition, suffering and secularity, and they relate the unity of God to the diversity, the tragedy and the autonomy of the human situation. How does this Lordship of the worlds contain, as it were, the pluralisms of existence, its sorrows and its arguable self-sufficiency?

The first of these is the religious problem of the emotional love of the natural order and all its ways and wonders, the problem of the imagination in worship. The world of phenomena is irreducibly plural and manifold. Our context of human experience, of love and sense awareness, is endlessly rich and diverse. This manifoldness, of course, lies at the root of superstition. It inspires the creation of images, to capture its delights or lay its fears. It is the source of nature worships, and of the language, the metaphors, the myths, by which men respond to it.

The doctrine of the unity of God is not meant to exclude this manifold. Rather the Qur'ān embraces it in the concept of "the signs of God," evocative of gratitude and wonder. All things may be celebrated, but only God is to be adored. Yet it is supremely difficult not to depreciate, or even atrophy, the register of cognizance of nature and of life in its fulness, if the doctrine of unity is stern and sharply hostile to the imagination. Conversely, there is a danger of idolatry implicit in all alertness to the external manifold. There is the temptation to stop at things and not pass through them to God. Do we not need myths and imagination, mind-pictures, word-pictures, if we are to possess the wonder? Yet may not these, by their very efficacy, divert the mind and heart from the God they affirm?

The Islamic doctrine of the unity of God, and its correlative, the menace of *Shirk,* or deification, have demanded the prohibition of all representational art. In the realm of worship Islam enforces, often with a puritan severity, a total veto on artistic joy in shape and image, music and iconography. Color, design, the craftsman's skill—these had to be reserved only for "religious" objects in the mosque, for lamps and tiles, for the margins of Qur'āns and for calligraphy. There could be no reproduction of the delightsomeness of flesh and blood, or form and body. This is the more notable in that, on the social plane, Islam is not, traditionally, ascetic, but rejoices in the physical benedictions of life.

The reason, of course, lies in the intense anti-idolatry necessary in the context of its genesis. Yet the problem remains. How is the worship of God alone properly to harness and reflect the endlessly plural benisons of His world and His creation? Nature cults, fertility rites, plural shrines—in a word, idols—are all rightly anathema. They arrogate from God the glory due to Him alone. But how, in a proper jealousy for that glory, do we conserve and articulate the love, the gladness, the wistfulness, the intimacy of dependence, the nearness of soul, which breathe in ignorant and "primitive" idolatries? How do we feel and move, as "unitarians," within the plural world, keeping the poetry of nature, but excluding the partializing superstition? How do we come by a worship that no longer suspects art, and by a love of the manifold which is not tempted to idolatry?

In all this Islam is close to a deep and perennial problem in the religious life of man. It is no less so in the second problem of the compatibility with Divine unity of the mystery of evil and suffering in the experience of man. If we affirm a sovereignty that is all-knowing, all-powerful, all-merciful and unrivalled, what are we to say of the burden of tragedy and wrong that weighs upon our whole history?

We have already heard the theologians insisting that there are no obligations in God, no laws of His nature by which He is bound. Yet the Qur'ān declares that "he has written down for Himself mercy." (Surah 6:12). Faith in the rule of God surely involves what is sometimes called a "theodicy," a justification of God in face of the reality of evil. The Islamic notion of *Ẓulm,* to which earlier reference has been made, includes the theme of "things which ought not so to be." The root idea in the term is out-of-place-ness, insubordination, defiance of right, or things—in a notable New Testament phrase—"standing where they ought not." What then are we to say about the reign of God in the light of the pretensions, the challenge to it, of the wrongs in life?

In the main, because of its emphasis on the transcendent, Islam ignores or neglects or does not hear these questions. It simply sustains its affirmation of God, of His unity and power, and its belief in His sublime immunity. It does not find a theodicy necessary either for its theology or its worship. On the practical and social level, wrong is to be identified, disowned and reversed by dint of the education and the discipline of the human community in a true *islām*. The ultimate mystery must not be understood to trouble heaven or the theologian.

What, then, finally, is the ultimate significance of the Islamic sense of "the Lord of the worlds"? It is a passion against all usurpation. It is the conviction that wrong worship is the sum of evil, that power, or race, or state, or creed, improperly exalted above God, spell the human wasteland. It is a perpetual warfare against all false absolutes. Only in the truly worthy truly recognized can human benediction lie. In the negative, it is a constant warning: "There is no god . . ."; in the positive a supreme assurance: ". . . except God."

In the deepest ways, therefore, it bears the full brunt of the contemporary secular challenge to the religious view of man and the world. As the most insistent and uncomplicated Divine charter for human life, its forthright theism means "theonomy," not autonomy, for humanity. Revelation Divinely given, law Divinely ordained, duty Divinely ordered, bring the sovereignty of heaven directly into all human business. The structure of obligation is authoritarian, statutory and inclusive. Every issue, every situation, returns to God and leads back to an obligation theologically constituted. Islam, in these ways, might be said to be programmatic religion *par excellence*.

What, then, of present assertions of human self-sufficiency, for which theism is no longer philosophically feasible, morally tolerable, or religiously desirable? What of man's alleged ability to dispense with the Divine hypothesis, in the adequacy of his own management of the world? What of his contrasted mood of futility and misgiving, prompting him to opt out of an existence with whose pointlessness and disorder he will have nothing to do?

For these disqualifications of its surest conviction about God Islam has answering resources. It is true that on the ordinary level Islamic thought has not yet squarely met these current secular pleas either of arrogance or despair. It is also true that in practice much secularity has invaded Muslim law and society, and that some conformity is sustained more by political and cultural emotion than by spiritual confidence. Nevertheless it teaches man both the boldness and the humility of the true iconoclast. It sees man as called to identify and dethrone the false gods, and able to do so. This, in the ultimate sense, *is* the meaning of the only proper autonomy. In so far as current "religionlessness" is such a dethroning, Islam, implicitly, is with it. It has always made idols its central negation.

But, immense tribute as this freedom to be idolatrous and this duty to be anti-idolatrous are to the dignity of man, the evident corollary of both is that he is called to, and fulfilled in, the true worship. There *is* an autonomy, but only for the sake, and in the way, of the ultimate submission. To cope with both the validities and the pretensions of secularity we can find all that we need in the single truth of the dual Islamic conviction: "There is no god . . . except God."

This chapter has set in review the main themes of the religion of the rule of God. God is "Lord of the worlds," Creator, Ordainer, Sustainer, and Disposer. "The excellent Names" serve a religious temper by also deterring a theological presumption. Whether in nature, or history, or aesthetics, or ethics, we find the same dominating concern for God over all, and the same tension, actual or potential, with the tumultuous factors in human affairs. The indictment against *Shirk* defends the sovereignty of God from all competitive challenge. Within the whole, there is the unresolved issue of how the Divine majesty and authority relate to the actualities of sin and wrong.

All these, the last most of all, must now be studied in the shape and in the policy of original and traditional Islam as history knows them. The *Shahādah* has its second clause: "Muḥammad is the apostle of God."

Quranic Passages to Study

Surahs 10:1 to 19; 13:1 to 18; 24:35 to 44; 59:19 to the end. Surahs 112; 113; 114.

Some Questions

1. What is the meaning of *islām* (small 'i')?
2. "Seek simplicity and distrust it." Would this be proper comment on the theology of Islam?
3. How does Islam understand "the excellent Names" of God?
4. Why the doctrine of the Divine unity?

2. *Muḥammad and the Rasūliyyah*

The formidable looking title word is simply the abstract noun from *Rasūl,* the credal description of the status role of Muḥammad, for which there is no precise or satisfactory English equivalent. The center of interest in this chapter is the vocation of Muḥammad in its personal and religious aspects, as a focal point of profound themes of truth and power, of revelation and response, of the word and the deed, leaving to the following chapter the scriptural corollary of that vocation, the Qur'ān, as the source book of law and theology, the textbook of faith and the manual of devotion.

When we search for a word to convey either the "doer" or the "doing" within the root verb about "sentness" we are in a difficulty. "Prophet" translates another and different word, denoting what is in general taken to be a relatively inferior station. Moreover, prophets, at least in the highest Biblical tradition are politically powerless as the necessary condition of their ministry and their integrity. They face establishments without displacing them, as Jeremiah so heroically exemplified. "Messenger" may do, but in popular English it is rather a minimal word, suggesting a negligible errand. "Apostle" also works, but is associated too much with Christian notions. New Testament apostles are always in relation to Jesus, as teacher and savior. They are only "apostles" for God by their relation to Christ. Muḥammad has no such derived ministry through a master: he is directly and immediately "apostled" to God Himself. The Qur'ān as Scripture comes only to him: it has penmen other than himself but does not come from their pens, nor is it *about* him. "Herald," "emissary," even "commissioner," would all possibly serve, were they not encumbered by associations that are too sentimental or too vulgar.

Rasūliyyah, the state of being sent, is essentially a juncture of message and mission, an affirmation with an imperative, a meaning that is to be declared, not a private awareness of truth, nor a publicity that has no roots in duty and urgency. It is communication acting by the energy of what it tells, and it is this event proceeding in and by a human personality instrumental to it. Muḥammad, says the creed, is *Rasūl Allāh:* the *Rasūliyyah,* we may safest say, is what it confesses. If this seems enigmatic, we go on to explore it on several levels empirical, psychic and spiritual. But first it must be acknowledged as the central historical element in the genesis and the significance of Islam.

There are in fact in Islam no paradigmatic events other than this one, no corporate and communal happenings which take their place in the definition and imagination of the faithful as constitutive of their religious being. The Old Testament turns on the pivot of the Exodus as the formative event, as memory takes it in the mythic expression of history—the Exodus, with Sinai and the Covenant and the Law. Christianity takes definition from the Cross and the Resurrection, highly singular events to be sure, yet embodying in their reception a deep, collective experience of newness of life and of salvation through suffering, incorporating the society of faith. Both these, and other, related faith events like the Exile, make the paradigm, or representative crisis, from which the character of the religion is determined. The *Rasūliyyah* of Muḥammad is the one such event in Islam, or, in different language, the Qur'ān is the only miracle. We must find the religious clue to Islam in the mystery of Muḥammad, recognizing that it is singular and unique. Revelation, as an experience belonged to him alone. But the Scripture he received communicates the message, and this in turn may be taken to oneself by memorizing and recital. From the page it may live in one's lips and heart. What it meant, in the receiving, was the private awareness of Muḥammad. There is continuity, in some sense, between what happened to Muḥammad and the role of earlier prophets, back to Abraham. But these kinships are not projected into the future and there is no vicarious participation in their essence. Muḥammad is "the seal of the prophets" with whom revelation ends in climax.

There are several different levels on which the historian may tell that story. In its barest terms, a man named Muḥammad, son of 'Abdallāh, born around 570 A.D., within a minor branch of the Quraish of Mecca, a pilgrim center of the Hijāz in western Arabia, began near the age of forty to preach in the city of his birth about the unity of God and judgment on idolatry, prompted, he said, by Divine commission so to do. After initial misgivings, he developed a powerful crusade in this cause, but recruited relatively few followers and little influential response. The opposition he encountered from the majority of his fellow citizens deepened from mild irritation to sharp antagonism. Whereupon he seized a favorable opportunity, migrated with his community to the city of Yathrib, to the north, later called Medina, which he brought increasingly under his control, involving its resources and people in armed struggle in the cause of Islam, until after several skirmishes and by wise manipulation of alliances and interests, he was able to bring the former capital to heel and establish a religio-political state under his complete authority through most of the Arabian peninsula. Throughout this whole activity, the revelations which had initiated his apostleship continued in intermittent sequence, directing his words and policies and giving dogmatic and legal patterns for the community. These ended just before his death in 632, when his achievement was complete and his work poised for perhaps the most dramatic eruption into general history that obscure beginnings ever attained.

It is important to measure the political dimensions of this concise and factual narrative, for they dominate the history and temper of Islam. Islamic origins did not coincide with a strong and rigorous military imperialism, like that of Rome in the first Christian century. On the contrary, the place and time of their first history still awaited effective unification of its chronic tribalism and its tradition of divisiveness. Efforts after unity, it is true, had been proceeding within Arab society in the decades immediately prior to Muḥammad's call. But the vital principle was still lacking, with the necessary quality of thrust and assurance to turn yearning into fact.

It was just this which the Prophet supplied. Tribal rivalries belonged with religious pluralism. To preach the unity of God against all territorial gods and nature-powers was to disclose the clue to human unity. But the victory of the message necessitated the overthrow of the *political* sanctions which sustained the pagan cults. Meccan idolatry had powerful vested interests, relating to the commerce and prestige of the city as guardian of the pagan pilgrim shrines. Hence the antagonism of their city-state to the person and word of Muḥammad—an antagonism sustained through thirteen weary years in ridicule, calumny and plot against him. The *Hijrah,* that is, "the emigration," by which he broke out of that impasse, involved the important, and new, principle of the priority of faith-allegiance over blood relationship. This revolutionary step gave clear warning to tribalism. Muḥammad saw himself immune from the obligations of non-belligerence in the months of tribal truce and reaped the benefit of the resultant surprise in his campaigns, shrugging off the opprobrium as merely incidental to the new order. After capitulation came magnanimity. It seemed right in retrospect to have broken truces which belonged to a system itself under repudiation, rather than to have failed effective unity. For, as the Qur'ān observes: "Sedition is more grievous than killing." (Surah 2:191). But then peace is better than chaos.

This story, however, with its emphasis on the political service of Islam is seriously incomplete, if the religious thrust is seen only as a gift-horse to the goal of unified rule. There has to be a third narrative to do larger justice to an honest whole. Islam could not have served these ends had it not been an end in itself. As such its crux in Muḥammad's story is vastly more profound than the foregoing.

As prophet-statesman, Muḥammad emerges as the exemplification of the deepest tension in religion. His vocation, as already narrated, was first puzzled, then thwarted, then burdened, by the mystery of antagonism. The inner conviction of prophethood by which he was energized and held to his course, in the ongoing revelation of Divine direction, ran into this reception of ridicule, scorn, rejection and conspiracy. How could this be borne? How should he resolve or even explain the enmity, without reneging on the vocation that aroused it? How might he maintain, still more vindicate, the commission in face of its public vilification, its cruel nonsuccess? Truth is great and prevails—but how? by what means and sinews? Does the business of witness enlarge to take in the duty of reckoning? At one stage the Qur'ān says explicitly: "Yours is the communicating: (*al-balāgh*), Ours [God speaking] is the issue, (*al-ḥisāb*)." (See Surahs 29:17; 24:53; 36:16; 42:47 and 13:40.) The patriarchal stories figure largely at this stage of the Qur'ān to reinforce the staying power of a sadly pressed Muḥammad. Yet fortitude under adversity was not their only quality. Did not the patriarchs come to manifest and outward triumph over their antagonists? Noah was certainly vindicated in the flood that drowned the taunting world, while Moses and David wielded supreme powers. The conviction steadily grew upon Muḥammad that he, too, should expect a similar vindication and enjoy authority as the means to it.

So, through the vicissitudes in Mecca, between 609 and 622, A.D., between his initial call and the climax of the *Hijrah,* he pondered the shape of prophetic duty and concluded it must involve statehood and warfare in the service of its truth and in the interests of its success. It did not suffice to send followers into the safety of Ethiopia, as he did in 615 A.D. He must seek an establishment where he might himself be master and whence he might bring to submission the stubbornness of his Meccan foes. The vision on Mount Ḥirā', it is true, had said only: "Arise and warn . . . recite in the name of thy Lord." But wrestling by words for that mission in the markets of Mecca had kindled the assurance that rule and strength of arm must be invoked, if the cause was not to fail. Religion must not evade the political realm: it needs its forces and by force must take it.

This task was the burden of Muḥammad's years in Medina. It hinged on two critical battles and the pacification which garnered their results. The Battle of Badr (624 A.D.) and the Battle of Uḥud (625 A.D.) were fought with the Meccan enemies. In the first Muḥammad gained a resounding success and his purpose gathered momentum. The Qur'ān calls it: "the day of the sign of favor." Uḥud was a more ambiguous encounter. But success crowned both Muḥammad's arms and his diplomacy, and eight years after his exile Mecca received him as its conqueror.

But this third narrative still does not suffice us. The historian has still not done justly by the Prophet. To say that a man began to preach, and all else followed by an inner logic, is to tell a fact and conceal the truth by so barely telling it. Where was that *Rasūliyyah* born? To answer: "In the will of God" is theological; "in the genius of Muḥammad" interpretative; "in the core of mystery" evasive. We are bound to seek the spiritual answer, by which "God" and "genius" and "mystery" may be related. If Muḥammad's vocation reacted in the ways we have described in sequel, to what was his vocation itself responding in its genesis?

It is customary to dub the pre-Islamic times "the *Jāhiliyyah* or, "the days of ignorance." Tradition's later picture of them is piously overdrawn and conflicts with immediate evidence from the Qur'ān itself and, indeed, from the pre-Islamic poets with their Arab virtues of manliness and courage. The term *Jāhiliyyah* is not simply "ignorance," in the sense of utter benightedness, but rather that stubborn unruliness we have already noted—a kind of insubordination that defies both single worship and a peaceful society. Even so, it was not an altogether unrelieved condition. There were already the *Ḥanīfs,* to whom the Qur'ān refers, men of the mold of Abraham, discontented with disunity and reaching after purer faith. Their apparent revulsion from idols may have stemmed from Jewish and Christian influences. These were certainly considerable in various parts of Arabia, though probably slightest in the immediate environs of Mecca. In the north and south of the peninsula, in pockets in the Medinan region, their traditions were familiar. The Ghassānids and the Lakhmids—tribes in the border areas to the north—were Christian peoples and there were churches in Najrān. These communities of Biblical monotheism, however compromised from its fullness, in circumstances we need not here explore, were probably accessible to Muḥammad.

Among their characteristics, the most impressive was the possession of Scriptures. "People of the Book" is a recurrent Quranic phrase. If Muḥammad was yearning for a source of unity here was the proof of one. To have Scriptures, to be "scriptuaries," was to constitute a people. For some reason the existing Scriptures did not suffice, had not sufficed, to fulfill the need within the Arab soul and Arab society. Perhaps it was that their communities were too possessive of them, or, in the case of the Jews, too insistently distinctive. Neither in fact, nor in intention, nor yet—it would seem—in translation, were they Arabic Scriptures. A book for the Arabs would have to be a new departure, extending, indeed finalizing, the principle, but in independence and distinction.

Hence, it would appear, came the germinal idea of "an Arabic Qur'ān"—the phrase with which the Scripture of Islam carefully describes itself. (See Surahs 12:2; 20:113; 41:3; 42:7; and 43:3 and pp. 31 f. below.) With the need came the instrumentality. Muḥammad seems to have come to vocation by this road, to have grown from an initial summons to recite into a conviction that by the sequence of his obedience a Scriptural *corpus* of heavenly deliverances was steadily realizing a book on earth—in the tongue of his own people.

Already before his fortieth year he had formed the habit of withdrawal to mountain retreats, to a cave or hillside, to brood and pray, away from Mecca's pagan confusions, its idol shrine and milling pilgrims, its busy merchants and rhyming poets—though these last, with their subtle skills and pleasing arts seem to have both fascinated and repelled him.

At an early point the Qur'ān refers to him as the "enmantled one" "enwrapped in robes," and the terms become in fact the titles of two of its chapters (Surahs 73 and 74). These are certainly not, at that point, the mantles of power it has in mind. Could they be, simply, the garments of a discipline of contemplation, the technique even of a mystic's search for illumination? Can we assume, in Muḥammad's own experience, something at least of the patterns later followed by Islamic mysticism, known as Sufism, in the centuries beyond? Such patterns of self-abstraction require, and serve, a cutting off of the sense world so that, undistracted, the spirit may await the visitation of the word. A cloak over the head makes a kind of tented abeyance of sight and sound, and the silence—to vary the imagery—spreads a sail for the wind of the Spirit. Was this the "enmantled" condition the Qur'ān means us to understand?

"Technique" is no doubt an alien word in this whole context, suiting more the instincts of an inquisitive science than the imponderables of a religious genesis. But when the initiation happened, when the words that were to become the earthly Qur'ān began to be heard and uttered by Muḥammad, what more fitting than that it should excel in native eloquence and be "an Arabic Qur'ān"? The authority of language and the rhythm of words—these were the joy and genius of Muḥammad's people, only that lyrical beauty deserved a better cause than loves and feuds. By the different inspiration of heaven, the native tongue should be the medium of their saving oracles: hence, it would seem, the careful insistence with which the Qur'ān repudiated the charge of mere poetry and imitation, yet claimed a surpassing eloquence.

The sense of vocation, then, and the genesis of a Scripture came in one event and moved together in parallel progression—Muḥammad, the recipient soul and voice of a Divine revelation, and the Qur'ān, the book of that recipience, gathering towards a whole in the movement of his prophetic action. "Recite in the Name of thy Lord . . . " runs the opening of Surah 96, which may well be also the opening of the entire book. The imperative verb *iqrā'* means to utter the given word, not extempore preaching, not private perusing of a silent text. "The voice said 'Cry.' " To the question: "What shall I cry?" came, for Muḥammad, the answer of a steady, if intermittent, sequence of deliverances, moving with the vicissitudes of his own career, with guidance, direction, vindication, illumination, and instruction, through the successive events by which Islam was launched and achieved. The documentary aspects await the next chapter.

Is the picture of Muḥammad now complete? The careful historian will probably ponder one further enquiry. Within this factual, political, social, and religious event in its composite unity, what manner of man was Muḥammad himself? "Charisma" is perhaps the word we must finally employ. Let it be clear that—for all the subsequent appropriation of the Prophet by the Muslim centuries as paragon and hero—these essential factors belong with the immediate history. They are not the formulation of a later reverence. The shape of his place in history was fashioned in his lifetime. Traditions, as we shall shortly see, grew voluminously around his legacy. But it was as a living presence, not as a legacy, that the achievement of Muḥammad abides in history. "Charisma" seems the right word even if it hides what it also tells. By some mystery of personal quality or authority of soul and force of will, he became that to which all else is commentary. In the Meccan/Medinan milieu of many gods and of wistful, turbulent men, Muḥammad toiled and strove in a single politico-religious vocation, inwardly assured and at length outwardly triumphant as the *Rasūl* of God.

Uncompromising as was its inner confidence and its use of power, that *Rasūliyyah* stays within its own bounds. The dignity did not need or receive the doubtful support of lavish manners or gratuitous pretension. Nor did it proceed by cringing adulation. And it resolutely precluded all notions of divinization. There was a radical way with hostility and a quite unhesitating assurance of the paramountcy of the cause over traditional mores or tribal conventions if these obstructed its path. Though in a spiritually perilous way, as we must observe, the office and the person were identical, the latter was wholly subdued to its understanding of the former. It is notable that the Qur'ān uses the personal name, Muḥammad, on only four occasions. One (33:40) has to do with the fact that he had no male heir, and another (3:138) is in the context of the general mortality of all prophets.

The same concern to have only the status which revelation gave made him eager to disavow all literary competences. It was a matter of importance that he be clearly dissociated from all professional versifiers, and when such connections became a taunting accusation they were vigorously denied. He was "the unlettered prophet," *al-nabī al-ummī*—apostle to those who had no Scriptures, but himself pretending to no prior skill in verse or oratory. The Qur'ān is to be seen as more certainly God's for being manifestly not his own.

Subsequent centuries, however, have tended to forget or to ignore the steady realism of the events themselves. There *is* a posthumous Muḥammad, the apostle in later tradition, the axis of mystical devotion. There were, broadly, three consequences for posterity in the *Rasūliyyah*. They were the political, the cultural, and the emotional.

The political is the Caliphate. When death claimed the *Rasūl,* in 632 A.D., his community was already a state and was about to become an empire. His demise had consummated the Scriptures of Islam: it might well have undone the state, for Muḥammad had been everything within it. The answer, prompt and timely, was the Caliphate, the office and dignity of successor to Muḥammad. The word *khilāfah* means simply following after and so filling the room of another. It did not include revelation, for the Qur'ān was now ended and could have no other instrument. But the springs of authority, the tasks of public leadership—these were committed to the successor, first Abū Bakr, then 'Umar, both fathers-in-law of Muḥammad, beginning an institution which continued, through many toils, down to 1924. It was a practical answer to a practical need. The theory developed after the fact. It has no explicit authority from the Qur'ān. But necessity and tradition sustained it for thirteen centuries as the legal, juridical form in which Muḥammad's rulership, his administrative, military, judicial, and other functions in the community, were given into other hands. We shall meet it again in discussing the community (*Ummah*) of which, until the last half century, it was an indispensable symbol.

But the gap at the Prophet's departing was not merely governmental. The Qur'ān, it is true, was complete. His death did not abruptly cut it off, for he had received its final sentences to crown his life. But that fact, so to speak, sacramentalized the heavenly silence. It was now over to the memorizers, the keepers by heart, the copyists. But they were serving a Book which was itself the seal of books of God. Men have to live beyond the last chapter of revelation, and what may be dogmatically complete is emotionally daunting. In these circumstances what was more natural than that they should turn to the memory of their mentor. What sounder reliance than the man upon whom God had relied?

So there came about in the sequel to the Qur'ān's finality the birth of tradition. All the areas of life for which the Scripture provided no guidance must be subdued to the exemplariness, the recollected habits, the preferences and anticipations of the Prophet. Let him be the criterion. That word, in Arabic form, *furqān,* was one of the titles of the Qur'ān itself. In Muḥammad's legacy of character and wisdom, as devout posterity remembered or conceived it, would be found its surest commentary and enlargement.

The growth in this way of a vast body of traditional lore about Muḥammad is one of the most remarkable phenomena in religious history. There is nothing quite like it outside Islam. Much of its content, as criticism of tradition readily allows, is extraneous to the real Muḥammad and comes into Islam from custom, law and sentiment encountered by the new religion in its rapid expansion in the two centuries after his death. But the important thing is that it came that way, with that imprint. Islam was not merely hospitable to accretions from without. It claimed them as the Prophet's own. And what was originally his own it enlarged, interpreted and applied, with meticulous concern for his approval. Thus Muḥammad reigned from the grave over the imaginations, the legislation, the daily life and personal habits of his community. Tradition became the second source of law, complementing the Quranic and extending its scope.

The impulse to find new law made legists the main group in the task and science of tradition-collecting. Given the religious authority over the whole of life, their search covered an immense territory of material down to the minutiae of personal hygiene and social behavior. It also covered a wide territory of travel. For such was the devotion to authenticity in traditions that their recorders across the lands of Islamic empire required themselves to join their own citations of example to the testimony of the last reporter in person, and thus backward to the immediate contemporary, or "companion," of Muḥammad, whose eye or ear had noted the original action or opinion. Attestation was primarily by the soundness of this chain (*isnād*) of reporting, rather than by the content or inherent credibility of the substance (*matn*) of the tradition. The science of biographies and movements relating to these bearers of traditions in their sequence became one of the major items of Islamic erudition. The canonical editors of the third Muslim century (800 A.D.) are among the most esteemed figures in its history.

It must be clear that the "virtue" by which Muḥammad filled this role was carefully distinguished from his Qur'ān recipience. That state of revelation (*waḥy*), usually denoted by certain external symptoms which became habitual, was one thing. The residual authority by which his talk, his *obiter dicta,* his example, came to be held as inspired and law-affording was another thing. Tradition did not confuse the unique status of the Quranic transactions that had occurred under the special aegis of the Divine. The tradition-yielding was a more general and diffused quality of his person, accruing, as it were, from the immense honor of his prophetic vocation. For its legal and religious role God had left ample occasion in the areas where the Qur'ān itself had been silent. Both the needs and the piety of the community saw that it was filled.

It was natural that ensuing time and widening spheres should make heavy demands upon the Prophet's posthumous directives thus recounted. But the lengthening years, of necessity, shifted the onus for new directions on to a communal consensus (*ijmāʿ*) beyond fields which could ever, even by deference, be linked historically with his person. Even then, however, consensus was complementary to tradition and relied heavily upon it for precedent and argument.

While tradition-finding continued up to the time of the great sifters and editors of the ninth century, Al-Bukhārī, Muslim, Ibn Mājā Al-Tirmidhī and others, there was, already, in some measure, this element of interaction between the Prophet (*Rasūl*) and the community (*Ummah*), between the repute and the pride that cherished it. It was not simply that Muḥammad shaped their patterns; it was also that their ideals shaped his image. He was the focus of their possessive satisfaction, the epitome of their ideology. Muḥammad's role in Islamic history thus exemplifies the religious necessity of concreteness, and the urge to find ideology embodied superlatively in a figure who is then corporately, even aggressively, possessed and set beyond all other comparison. It might perhaps be called in this Islamic form "religious mentorship." Its sanction lies in its holding all values in terms uniquely proprietory to one's own community. "Where we like, we liken" is a rule not only for language in the making of metaphors, but for faiths in the making of their souls.

This consideration merges into the third aspect of Muḥammad's role in history, earlier described as the axis of devotion. Muslims as legists had the stake we have described in the Prophet's memory. But as well as lawyers there were saints and seekers. Muḥammad had sternly forbidden all veneration. Together with the Jesus of the Qur'ān, and all the prophets, he was strictly and only a servant. The battle he had for Divine unity was at all times preoccupied with the menace of Divine "association"—partners with God, deifications, and divinization—all deadly dangers to the purity of faith and the proprieties of truth. Of no such travesty could Muḥammad ever be guilty. This fidelity was never in doubt.

Yet, in his vocation, he had been, operatively, very close to God. Allāh and the *Rasūl* were bracketed, inseparably, in the *Shahādah* or witness of faith. Throughout the Qur'ān there is a steady reiteration of the juncture between the concerns of God and of the Prophet. The range and frequency of this has a quite terrifying quality for those to whom it is not axiomatic. It far outdoes any temper the reader meets and shrinks from in the Psalms, where the psalmist's interests—and enemies—are assumed to coincide with God's. "Your patron is God and his apostle" (Surah 5:60). "We believe in God and his messenger and we obey" (24:40). "God and his messenger spoke the truth" (33:22). "Obey God and obey his apostle and dispute not with one another lest your power departs" (8:45),—an allegiance about which there is no room for debate. The converse is equally adamant. "Those who disobey God and his messenger, theirs is the fire of hell" (72:24). The bounty that enriches is both God's and Muḥammad's (9:75). Throughout, there is this close, intimate linking of both, in respect of claims to loyalty, threats against treachery, rewards, and promises. All alike come from the twin source. Here is one of the sharpest religious problems of the whole Qur'ān. For it seems to jeopardize the very sovereignty, undivided and singular, for which Islam stands. Yet *islām* is its justification. The absolute tends to absolutize whatever serves it and so endows the service with its own absolutism. All the Joshuas, the inquisitors, the Divine-righters of history, pass this way.

The Quranic situation certainly intends only instrumentality, and argues that it is precisely instrumentality which makes it what it is. The dilemma is deep and it is there symbolically when the worshipper enters the mosque and notes the two large, equal circles or discs high on the walls, where the single words Allāh and Muḥammad are set, in clear script, as the foci of his thought. That context of the mosque and spirituality is where this third dimension of Muḥammad's meaning for Muslims must be understood.

It is, emphatically, association without *Shirk*. In orthodox Islam, Muḥammad has no mediatorship and no suprahuman status. The *Rasūliyyah* confers great dignity, but no divinity. Popular devotion, however, acclaims it with its own emotions and instincts, which strict theology has been unable to repress. Early in the sequence of traditions, stories multiplied of the Prophet's infancy and youth, of prenatal signs and portents and of miraculous elements in his biography. The Qur'ān lends some limited support to the last—though the passage may be taken figuratively—in the allusion to the night ascent to heaven via the "farthest mosque" in Jerusalem. (Surah 17:2 f). But it was overwhelmingly tradition and pious instinct, not the Qur'ān, which developed this Muḥammad of miracle and wonder.

Of greater significance was the spiritual cult of Muḥammad's person and character as bridging, so to speak, the divide between the awful majesty on high and the struggling frailty below. There grew in Shī'ah Islam[1] an intense devotion to the Prophet's family, to 'Alī—cousin and son-in-law, to Ḥasan and Ḥusain—grandsons, and the line which so precariously survived the massacre of Karbalā'. Out of political failure, the Shī'ah cause became the ground of a passionate devotion to the lineal family of the Prophet, the *Āl* of Muḥammad, hallowed by the bitter tragedy of martyrdom and emotionally sharpened by the suffering of external failure. Sunnī Islam, with its accent on the community of believers, its external success and its dogmatic rigorism, rejected these Shīʿah emotions as disloyal and perverse.

To reject them, however, was not to escape the religious yearnings to which they related. For all their emphasis on solidarity, on law and sound tradition, on realism and nondeviation, Sunnis also needed to possess Muḥammad in terms satisfying to the springs of personal religion. From one angle, their very antipathy to Shīʿah positions accentuated cultic trends in their own Sunnī direction. Muḥammad's legacy, however well entrusted to tradition and to law, could not live in a devotional silence. It could not be left only with pundits. Alongside the ritual prayer, or *Ṣalāt,* to which all Muslims were bound, went a popular incorporation of Muḥammad into acts of devotion. With the help of ambiguity in a pivotal verse, his intercession was sought and believed. (Surah 2:255 asked: "Who is there that will intercede with Him save by his leave?" and it was argued that leave would be given to Muḥammad.) Petition, eulogy, celebration all came to be offered in his name. The position his example enjoyed with the moralists, his person filled for the worshippers. The *Rasūliyyah* that had been the highway of the word from God to men became the highway of many words from men to God.

This development owed much to the encouragement it received from a single verse in the Qur'ān. Surah 33:56 reads: "God and his angels celebrate the Prophet. O ye who believe celebrate him and greet him with peace." The word here translated "celebrate" means "to pray" and is so used in respect of the ritual "praying" or *Ṣalāt,* to be studied in Chapter 5. God cannot, of course, be said to "pray." The word, in origin meaning "to bow," has then the sense of recognition or commendation. It is a sort of heavenly *Magnificat* in 33:56. "My Lord magnifies his soul: my Maker rejoices with his spirit." "Send down, or invoke, blessing upon" is a frequent rendering. Help can be had from the converse in 33:57. "Those who speak evil of the prophet . . ." where the sense is to "malign."

God, then, "blesses" Muḥammad and the believers do likewise. This is known as *Taṣliyah,* a technical noun derived from the verb. It is closely linked with *Taslīm,* or the invocation of peace: "Greet him with peace," and this lends support to the idea that the whole phrase may have to do with an inviolability of the Prophet, a sort of Hosanna: "God save Muḥammad" which is at once fact and invocation. There *may* in this context be a purely practical sense, namely vindication against detractors; so say some modern exegetes. But it is much more likely to be, as it is popularly taken, a kind of reverent, celestial Hurrah!

Heaven rejoices in Muḥammad, and the faithful echo Divine approval. Men salute him whom God perpetually attests. Here devotion found abundant opportunity. Mysticism took ready incentive, as we will see in the chapter on Liturgy, not only from the Prophet's example of meditation, but from the idea of his oneness with the Divine mind. He was the Aḥmad (a variant of Muḥammad) without the "m"—meaning he was *Aḥad* or the One, a title of

Allāh. Or he was "the 'Arab" without the "A" that is, *Rabb* or Lord. He was the very Divine *Ṣalāt* in the *miḥrāb,* or niche, of the Divine being, the eternal joy of God in the reality of His revelation—a concept perhaps loosely comparable with that of personified wisdom in the Book of Proverbs: "I was daily His delight . . . " The obvious tension of these mystical ideas, and the practices they sanctioned, in conflict with the orthodox dogma, did not prevent them from playing a prolonged and major role in the religious prosperity of Islam.

Popular faith possessed Muḥammad with less subtlety but no less fervor. Poems on his birthday, *Maulid* songs and processions, invocations of his name, and celebrations of the episodes of his life diffused through the centuries a sense of participation in heavenly things, a vicarious proximity to God in the supreme intermediary, the Prophet after God's own heart. The mention of his name and office in all pious writing or speaking is immediately followed by the formula: "Let the blessing and peace of God be upon him."

It must conclude this brief venture into the fact of Muḥammad within the house of Islam. There is much else to which a fuller study should give heed and some aspects will emerge under other themes that follow. It is, however, remote and academic to call it a formula. For those within it is a salutation of the heart, a greeting to the proven ways of God.

Quranic Passages to Study

Surahs 96; 97; 73; 74; 80; 68; 42; 109; 17: 84 to the end; 8:1 to 40; and Surah 110.

Some Questions

1. "Yours the word; Ours (God's) the issue." Consider Muḥammad's career in the light of this principle.
2. Explain the call of Muḥammad and explain his achievement.
3. What is the religious meaning of the "blessing" of Muḥammad?
4. In what ways does Muḥammad "belong to the ages"?

3.
Qur'ān

Our best point of departure in a study of the Qur'ān is from the fact of its being Arabic. In reflection on the career of Muḥammad we have noted the twin elements of Scripture possession as the clue to a people's cohesion or solidarity, and the fascination of poetic forms and freedom for Arab society. On both counts the Prophet's revelation is "an Arabic Qur'ān," responding both to the Arab love of language and to the Arab yearning for the unity a proper Scripture might bestow. "Had We made it a Qur'ān in an alien speech," observes an interesting conjecture in Surah 41:44, the foes of the preacher would have said: "If only its verses had been made plain to understand. Fancy! an uncouth tongue, and he an Arab!" Clearly pride of language, comprehension, propriety, all required that the Scripture should address its first and "native" people in the music of their own tongue.

But, by the same token, it is "an alien speech" to all those multitudes who come to it in the worldwide dispersion of its fame and mission. For them the obstacles are formidable indeed. They meet us at once in the simple but bothersome business of transliteration. Why not "Koran," which is a generally recognizable designation? The vowel "o," however, does not exist in Arabic and "k" is another consonant not used in this word. We have to make a choice between a distortion that happens to be current and a correctness that may be puzzling. Again, why "Qur'ān," and not "the Qur'ān" in the heading? A good enough reason, better clarified in the sequel, namely that there is a concept here as well as a book, something akin to "history" and "the history," or "news" and "the news." The Qur'ān by its own showing is also a Qur'ān: it finalizes an entity (revelation and recital) of which there are other examples.

But far more vexing than these elementary matters are the exacting ventures of translation proper. Let it be said at once that the difficulties are not insuperable. There are, after all, vastly more Muslims than Arabs. Persians, Turks, Pakistanis, Indians, Indonesians, Hausas, Malays, and scores of others have the Qur'ān at the center of their religious existence, with only a tiny fraction of their numbers, pundits and experts, able to reach it in the original Arabic. But, heartening as this thought is, the daunting and sober truth is that the Qur'ān is, in fact, untranslatable. The exasperation to which endless readers, Carlyle and Gibbon outspokenly among them, have been reduced in their struggle to appreciate the Qur'ān without Arabic, is no idle thing. It is honest fact and all the more teasing for the very sympathy that wanted to surmount it. The frustrations of patience are more disconcerting, faced with the obscurities that foreign translations often involve, than are the complaints of hostility. Resourcefulness and assurance over this problem can only grow from a frank and intelligent appreciation of its nature.

The Qur'ān's being untranslatable must be assessed from two angles, the dogmatic and the literary. The former is the more easily handled. It arises from the traditional and long-standing exegesis of the several passages, noted in Chapter 2, which insist: "We have sent it down an Arabic Qur'ān." The simple case here is that if God willed the Holy Book should be Arabic, it is no part of obedience or submission to turn it into any other tongue. There is a dogma, therefore, about the form as well as about the substance, and these are not separable. Revelation, we may say, is a linguistic as well as a spiritual phenomenon. The Scripture is a miracle of eloquence and diction, as well as the repository of final truth. Meaning cannot be assured in such sacred and crucial fields of truth unless language is also verbally inspired and given. Once given, in the revelatory particular, which is Arabic, it cannot be undone or transposed. Translation, even if successful in respect of content, deliberately destroys form, so that the result is, at best, only half of the original. It was for this reason that Marmaduke Pickthall, for example, as an English Muslim, in 1928 entitled his translation: *"The Meaning of* the Glorious Koran." For the title: "The Glorious Koran" could not rightly be given to any non-Arabic version. Others get over the difficulty by printing Arabic and the other language in parallel columns. The duty of the faithful is to honor the Divine mind that decreed the Arabicity and not seek to change either the one or the other.

However, there is one overriding consideration which, in our present context, suffices to terminate the long and often meticulous debate on this theme and to sustain the enterprise of translation as both loyal and desirable. It is the simple observation that in almost all the passages that refer to "an Arabic Qur'ān" intelligibility for the Arabs is the reason, explicit or implied, why it is so. "Perhaps you will understand," or "for a people who know . . . " or ". . . that you may warn the mother of the villages," namely, the metropolis of Mecca with its Arabic-speaking populace. The same note is sounded in the conjecture with which we began. An *'ajamī* Qur'ān, a Scripture other than Arabic, would not be decipherable. Such a "revelation" would be pure folly and empty mockery, being only a jingle of sound, a "barbarous thing."

But if the Arabic language of the Qur'ān is for its intelligibility to Arabs, then translation, where non-Arabs are involved, becomes imperative. Seen in this sense, the very passages, which justified orthodox persistence in the belief that only Arabic could be "Qur'ān," in fact imply a duty of translation, since otherwise the central intention, namely understanding, would be thwarted. Many other practical and rational factors have tended powerfully in the same direction, and the old reluctance now has a diehard and archaic kind of look. Translation, in fact, if not in unanimous theory, is everywhere conceded and undertaken. Many Muslims today urge that believers should not let this task go by default to unbelievers.[1]

The literary problem still remains. Translation is not merely a theme for debate among dogmatists. It is a strenuous enterprise for a painstaking scholarship, and one that can never be wholly satisfactory. The form and substance question just noted is greater as a concrete issue for translators than as a theoretical matter for theologians. Sense is closely wedded to words, and meaning to shape. The Arabic of the Qur'ān has its vocabulary subtleties, its cadences and rhymes, its metaphors and poetry. All these tax the ingenuity of the translator. It is almost impossible, in many passages, to avoid interpretation in translating. Hence the otherwise misleading title of much the best English version, A. J. Arberry's *The Koran Interpreted,* where the introduction may usefully be consulted for many of the technical problems incurred.[2] This translation is not, as its title might suggest, a commentary. But it concedes that there is a subtle quality which makes the Qur'ān outside Arabic no longer itself. All that English, or German, or any other language can do is to interpret that quality in another key.

This matter is, no doubt, common to all great literature. Shakespeare in French is as deplorable to an Englishman as Dante in another tongue is to the Italian. The indefinable quality of the native utterance becomes tame and flat in the new guise. The non-Arab, whether Muslim or westerner, has to keep always in view the impoverishment represented by his, albeit intelligible, version, as contrasted with the feel, the emotive power, the warm thrill of the original for its own heirs.

There are inviting vistas of poetry. Consider Surah 94, in Arberry's rendering—less inspired than usual:

> Did We not expand thy breast for thee
>   and lift from thee thy burden,
> the burden that weighed down thy back?
>   Did We not exalt thy fame?
>
> So truly with hardship comes ease; (repeat)
>   So when thou art empty, labour,
> And let thy Lord be thy Quest.[3]

Dawood's version, *The Koran,* runs as follows:

> Have We not lifted up your heart and relieved you of
>   the burden that weighed down your back?
> Have We not given you high renown?
> Every hardship is followed by ease. (repeat)
> When your task is ended, resume your toil, and
>   seek your Lord with all fervour.[4]

The English, in neither case, betrays the fact that there are here four and two terminal rhymes, two and two interior rhymes, as well as the refrain. But it would take freer paraphrase to attempt them in English and at best it could only be remote.

> Have We not lightened your heart
> Easing your guerdon,
> The frame's heavy burden,
> And lauding with honour your part?
> For pain of grief there's gain of peace (repeat)
> When steadied, be readied anew,
> And all your desire to be your Lord's.[5]

The Arabic refrain *maʿ al-ʿusri yusran* yields no such neat, sweet equal, and our feeble attempts at interior and final rhymes are still far away from the lilt and the metre of the original. We had better regret to be prosaic than strain to be poetic. For from that kind of hardship there is no ease.

The reader may multiply this sort of situation scores of times. Poetry aside, there are perplexities of grammar. For example, take the vital passage denying the actuality of the crucifixion of Jesus in Surah 4:157. "They did not kill him, they did not crucify him, but he (or it) was resembled to them." Translators have said the antecedent to the (hidden) pronoun "they" is "the Jews." Others suggest (with much less ground) that there is an intention of discrimination—not "these" but "those"; namely, it was the Romans who did it. Further, is the second (also hidden) pronoun "he" or "it"? Was Jesus made to be resembled by some other person—crucified, by this mistaken identity, instead of him? Or, was "it," namely crucifixion, only apparently accomplished, only seemingly done? It is impossible to decide these questions in an equivalent English sentence without implicit exegesis as well as actual translation.

Or again, there are elastic terms which themselves undergo development within the Qur'ān. The term, *fitnah,* for example, when it first occurs means a trial or test—the dangers of military service for a family man (See Surah 64:15). It later comes very close to "sedition," the menace that intrigue is to the established cause. In the latter case *fitnah* is the archenemy, which warfare has to liquidate, "in order that religion may be wholly God's"; in the former it is an emotion within the ranks which deters the will for the risk of battle.

Examples recur throughout the Qur'ān and they are more readily solved, or held in solution, when they are left in Arabic, than when, as translation usually requires, they have to be forced into resolution of their essential ambiguity.

But the other side of these matters is that their very presence is the token of the Quranic excellence in its original Arabic. We must pause to take this fact in its technical measure. Muslims believe in what is known as the *Iʿjāz* or *muʿjizah* of the Qur'ān—its matchlessness and incomparability. The terms mean that it cannot be rivalled in respect either of form or of worth. This superlative eloquence is regarded in orthodox circles as the crowning evidence of its Divine origin, the more so as it is found on the lips of a Prophet who disowned all poetic competence and was understood to be *ummī,* or "illiterate." We have seen earlier the more likely sense of this phrase as "the unscriptured" one. But it is widely understood as indicating actual inability to read or write and so to mean "the scripted" Prophet, that is, one who received what he uttered—just as a spokesman might from a text whispered to him in the wings—a text which is on his lips from a composing source outside himself. So the words and sequences of Quranic recital by Muḥammad follow the content of the book in heaven, "the preserved tablet" whence their phrasing, as well as their meaning, is drawn. Muḥammad is thus the mouthpiece of the preexistent Scripture, given to him in the experience of *waḥy,* or "revelation," which covers both substance and form.

This heavenly composition in the prophetic utterance is, accordingly, *sui generis,* incapable of being imitated. This uniqueness was made the theme in several places of a challenge to Muḥammad's foes and doubters. "Bring a surah like it": "bring ten surahs like it" if you are sincere. (See Surahs 2:23; 10:38 and 11:12). The incapacity of the Arab hearers—the challenge was not to foreigners—to match or better the Quranic eloquence has always been interpreted as attesting its indubitable worth and its heavenly origin. Therefore, eloquence is the only miracle and the sufficient one. The authority of the Qur'ān is religiously bound up with the incomparability of its language. That this aspect of its revelatory credentials is not accessible outside the Arab world does not affect, doctrinally, its universal relevance and its multilanguage destiny as revelation.

The most obvious recourse for the reader in search of the intelligible Qur'ān is the sense of chronology. What Muḥammad received in his claim to *Rasūliyyah* coincided, as we have seen, with a sequence of events through the twenty-three years of his prophetic life. What medieval exegetes called "the occasions of the descent [of the Qur'ān]," *asbāb al-nuzūl,* were the historical circumstances, the corporate or personal episodes, in relation to which the Qur'ān came, and in the light of which it had to be understood. The steady accumulation of the deliverances marched with the narrative evolution of his fortunes, in the developing roles, first of preacher, then of ruler. This accumulation was necessarily an experience which could not be expedited so as to anticipate events which had not yet emerged within the logic of his mission in its environment. The Qur'ān could not have been vouchsafed to him as a whole book at one time (Surah 25:32). In his understandable eagerness to receive more, Muḥammad is warned not to "hurry the recital." This directive could refer to hasty speaking but more likely means the desire to have totally what could only come gradually. The Qur'ān was given by God in instalments so that the Prophet may be duly upheld and the people progressively instructed (Surahs 17:106 and 75:16).

For this reason the criterion of chronology is built into the very structure and concept of the Qur'ān as a cumulative revelation. Unhappily, however, it does not dictate its actual arrangement. The Surahs, or chapters, after "the

Opener," are arranged, approximately, in order of diminishing length, from the longest (2) to the shortest (the last ten). Within themselves many of the longer Surahs are composite and belong to different points in the time sequence. Some exegetes, in their reluctance for contextual, as opposed to dogmatic, exegesis, hail this nonchronological arrangement of the Quranic canon as Divinely willed, though by this attitude they also deprecate, at least by implication, its historical setting. Others, of surer instinct and less timidity, strive to identify the precise sequence, and even to rearrange the whole accordingly.

The average reader simply has to cope as best he may with the handicap of this situation and might be well advised, in a rough and ready way, to begin at the end and move backwards to the start, knowing that thus he will be proceeding with the general run of the history. Or he may follow one of the several rearrangements ventured by different Muslim and western scholars.

The data for such chronological editions are readily at hand, even if they involve debate and divergence on particular points. The Qur'ān itself incorporates officially in its chapter headings the note *Makkiyyah* or *Madaniyyah* "at Mecca" or "at Medina." The *Hijrah,* on which the story of Muḥammad hinged, occupies, therefore, the same centrality for the Scripture. There are the revelations that are pre-*Hijrah* and those that are post-*Hijrah*. The watershed that gives the calendar its origin divides the book just as it defines the *Rasūliyyah*.

The ninety or so Surahs of the Meccan period (609 to 622 A.D.) and the twenty-four of the Medinan period (622 to 632 A.D.) can be further identified by characteristics belonging, in a fairly obvious way, with their setting in time. The former are often subdivided into early, middle and late Meccan. The early utterances are fervent, ecstatic, intensely poetic, ejaculatory, with their ardent themes of judgment impending and idolatry doomed. The passion and urgency of the first warnings and summons to faith and repentance slowly merge into more measured, argumentative, dialectical style and mood. The initial preaching, as we saw, runs into ridicule, opposition and disdain. Controversy develops. The Meccan hearers make charges of jinn-possession, madness, pretension, or deceit, which Muḥammad is directed to deny and rebuff. The Qur'ān, throughout the middle period, settles into prolonged contention, battling with the gibes. There is frequently the exchange: "They say . . . ," "Say thou . . . "; the charge and the answer. Poetry cannot be quite so vibrant and spontaneous in this setting. Controversy is its necessary second round.

In this general milieu comes, for the most part, the patriarchal material in which the Qur'ān parallels, in broad terms, the Old Testament figures. Their relevance seems to lie in two considerations. They provide patterns of fortitude by which Muḥammad may be encouraged, since most of them had to struggle against similar odds in the same idol-defying cause. But they also emerged to success and vindication. The Qur'ān does not speak of the tragic and brokenhearted prophets, of Hosea or Jeremiah. The bringer of the Arabic Scripture may thus be reassured as well as fortified. These narratives teach other lessons also, of providence and truth. They undergird the Quranic conviction that there is a unity within all Scriptures, however disloyal their preceptors may have been.

But just as intensity of poetry gave way to tenacity of witness, all within the same *preaching,* so, in turn, stouthearted utterance gives way to energetic action. We have already studied this inner decision of Muḥammad for the power structure that the *Hijrah* reaches towards and inaugurates. The *Jāhiliyyah* of resistance is not simply an ignorance to be informed, or a dullness to be illumined. It is also a stubbornness to be overcome, a perversity to be defeated. The Qur'ān naturally registers this fundamental shift from prophet to statesman, from preacher to ruler. Events, skirmishes, deputations, treaties, accessions, become more conspicuous as *asbāb al-nuzūl.* The text marches with the armies and moves with the public affairs of Medina. The legislative element becomes pronounced. The Surahs grow longer, argument recedes and authority dominates. Personal events in the life and entourage of Muḥammad assume an importance they did not have in Mecca. There develops what is apparently a much readier incidence of deliverances, without the anguish and soul-searching which belonged with the outset of the Qur'ān. The text is now involved in the superintendence of the life and order of a whole community, both in war and peace, in the social manifold of birth, marriage, divorce, inheritance, citizenship, taxation, ritual, and community. Some of the content of the Qur'ān in this dimension will meet us in Chapters 4 and 5. The translator's problems are, of course, correspondingly less exacting in this sphere. Prose, especially the lawmaker's, has much less to lose in another tongue than the exaltations of poetic fire. All the commentator needs is a sense of time and place and a legal head.

It is worth observing here that the Qur'ān has little reflection on general history beyond its intense interest in the transitoriness of human communities. It sees men as successors to one another in the flux of history, hastening their sheer mortality by their perversity. Retribution and requital, as well as natural transience, overtake the proud cultures and fabled empires of men. "How many a city have We destroyed for its evil-doing and now it is fallen on its very turrets" (Surah 22:44). There were the glories of south Arabia, nourished by the vast irrigation works around the town of Ma'rib whose collapse left an awesome memory in the tales of Muḥammad's people. There are fleeting references, also, to Alexander the Great in Surah 18:83, with his far-flung conquests, both eastward and westward, "the owner of the two horns" bestriding the earth. Surah 30 opens with a reference to a defeat of the Greeks by the Persians, the reversal of which is promised anon. This no doubt mirrors the protracted rivalries of Byzantium and Persia in the days before Islam.

For the rest, the sweep of universal history does not figure in the Qur'ān. Patriarchal narratives have their bearing on the Meccan scene. But the history that receives and "contextualizes" the revelation is within the single quarter century of the unique apostle and in the orbit of the twin cities that his mission embraced.

The canon of the Qur'ān, arising from the twenty-three years of Muḥammad's *waḥy,* took an even shorter period to receive definitive recension. For it was completed within the reign of 'Uthmān (d. 656). The Prophet's preaching and speaking within the Quranic state was assiduously repeated and loyally memorized by his followers. The very term "Qur'ān" applies equally to this recital of theirs as to his. Scholars generally hold that what he so delivered found its way, without serious loss or impairment or alteration, into the canon, and that extraneous material, lacking this double *imprimatur* of his uttering and theirs, his inspiration and their reception, did not. The things recited were inscribed, no doubt in different ways and places, consistently with their periodic character. It appears that Muḥammad used secretaries. These fragments steadily accumulated but do not seem to have been edited or incorporated into a volume before his death. Abū Bakr in 633 A.D. set the first recension under way. But twenty years later there had come to be diverse, even rival, texts, associated with different local centers and dialects. It was to obviate strife that 'Uthmān finalized and authorized one recension only—a step which in fact engendered deep dissension and contributed to the unrest and revolt which ended his rule. The canonization, however, stood, and the almost complete elimination of other copies foreclosed what might have been bitter controversies. Though many quests and questions remain for academic scholarship, the Qur'ān has a documentary uncomplicatedness akin to its authoritarian directness and simplicity.

What we have called the concentration of the Qur'ān in time and place needs to be seen, however, in the context of its belief in the long sequence of prophets and their scriptures. It is itself the last, not the solitary, Scripture. From Adam through to Jesus, prophets, teachers, and apostles came and went, bearing their message from God and their witness to men. They came "from God, reading purified pages comprising authentic books," to quote Surah 98:2. Adam gave the creatures names and so inaugurated all knowledge. Moses received the *Taurah,* David the *Zabūr* or Psalms, Jesus the *Injīl* or Gospel. Almost all the Biblical figures down to Elisha and Jonah are present in the Qur'ān, together with extra-Biblical names, Ṣāliḥ and Hūd and the intriguing Luqmān, or Aesop. These servants of the Divine will differed in the reach of their audience or the range of their message. Some had limited constituencies and only preparatory truths. All comes to its climax in the finalizing Qur'ān, the revelation that ends revelation. Muḥammad is the seal of the prophets, and the consummation of their wisdom.

So it is that in the Muslim view all the Biblical Scriptures should be consistent with the Qur'ān. When they are not so, it means that their custodians have tampered with them and distorted their contents, or that the final revelation has abrogated their provisions as being only a proximate stage on the way to truth. This assumption of corruption or of abrogation has, of course, been a provocative and taxing issue between Islam and the earlier monotheisms.

Some of the divergencies in the patriarchal narratives are only slight and concern emphases more than essence. They can readily be studied in the story of Joseph which, unlike the diffuse references, say, to Abraham, or Noah, or Moses, is concentrated in a single, orderly sequence in one Surah, the twelfth. But other aspects involve sharp controversies about the Bible arising within Muḥammad's own career. Notable among these are the covenant-election theme of the Old Testament and the Incarnation and the Cross of Jesus in the New, both of which the Qur'ān energetically denies.

There are, also, more subtle differences and disparities. Scriptures as the Qur'ān sees them, "come down" upon their servants, who recite their contents. They are the human iteration of the words of God. The concept of texts, even "sheets," or papers, *scripta,* is paramount. Revelation does not include human address to God, as in many psalms, nor the personal, autobiographical, travail of prophets. Nor is it the corporate experience of a community at large. Nor, again, is it in any sense the significance *per se* of a personality in a situation. The word is never made flesh to dwell: it is made speech to utter. Nor, again, is it the living commentary of a pastoral spirit on the sharp crises of existence, as these occur, for example, in the epistles of the New Testament. Epistles, on a Quranic view, can never be revelation, since they travel horizontally: they do not "come down."

Yet, for all these strenuous and indeed irreducible differences, there is deep importance in the Quranic idea of scriptural continuity. Some are ready to see in the Quranic view that every people has its messengers a possible validation of Hindu and Buddhist Scriptures also. Certainly, within the Judeo/Christian/Muslim sphere, there are many shared dimensions of faith. It is well not to allow the contentions to obscure how much is assumed in common and contested from common premises. If, to many, the Qur'ān's claim to supercession is distressing, it at least implies affinities that are by no means wholly negated and whose durability may at length affect the harshness of the enmity caused and returned.

One of the most striking of Quranic passages about God is in the Surah of Light (24):

> God is the light of the heavens and the earth.
> The likeness of His light is as a niche,
> Wherein is a lamp, the lamp in a glass, the glass like a glistening star,
> kindled from a blessed tree,
> An olive neither of the east nor of the west,
> Whose oil would almost shine had no fire touched it.
> Light upon light: God guides to His light whom He will:
> God brings similitudes for men and God has knowledge of all things.

It seems clear that niche and lamp and oil and light belong to a similitude of chapel and rite. For the verse goes on:

> (Light) in temples God has allowed to be raised up,
> Where His Name is commemorated,

Glorifying Him therein, morning and evening,
Men whom neither commerce nor trafficking
Diverts from the remembrance of God.

These discernible, interreligious features of the Qur'ān are not, here, directly, our concern. But our taking Surah 24 this way brings us to the whole question of exegesis in Islam. The centrality and finality of the Qur'ān make commentary a major field of theology and law. What, then, are the criteria to be applied to the understanding of the sacred text? Are exegetes free for the sort of conjecture we have just made, finding and proposing allusions which common sense or history suggest? How, in fact, has commentary proceeded in the long history of scriptural possession by Muslims?

The answers are, in part, implicit in what has been already indicated. The strictly scriptural nature of revelation has made for an extreme reverence for the letter. Grammar, vocabulary, construction, and case receive a meticulous attention. Parsing is the first obligation of the classical commentators. The dogma of "Arabicity" is taken to preclude search for the bearings of loan words from other languages, which might usefully indicate possible sources of Quranic background and provide clues to original meanings. If it is not conceded that there are non-Arabic words this field of enquiry is closed. The habit of continuous memoriter tends to keep devout response to the text close to the adjacent verses, as they stand in the reciter's sequence. It is often assumed that the nonchronological order has a Divine sanction—a belief that can discourage thematic cross-reference and even reduce concern for "the occasions of revelation."

These latter, however, come into their own in exegesis at least for the sake of exhortation or homiletics. Commentary draws heavily upon traditions, seeing that the stories from the Prophet's companions fill out details of events and situations in which Quranic history is involved. Citation of them helps to reinforce the moral guidance of the Qur'ān and is customary in the mosque sermon.

The most important single principle of commentary yielded by the Qur'ān itself is in Surah 3:7, which reads: ". . . the Book, some of whose verses are decisive, being of the essence of the Book, and others which are ambiguous." The following verses go on to suggest that the "ambiguous" verses attract dissidents and pretentious exegetes, who need to remember that finally "interpretation" is known only to God. The two crucial adjectives here, "decisive" and "ambiguous," mean, in the one case, clear, direct, unequivocal, perhaps even legal and precise, and in the other, metaphorical, analogical, figurative, allegorical, and parabolic. There is some doubt about what is intended in describing the former as "the mother of the Book," a phrase which is used elsewhere in the sense of the heavenly original, the celestial Book recited to Muḥammad that, by his recital, it might in turn be the revelation on earth. It is clear, at any rate, that both types of verse are integral to the Qur'ān, that it possesses clear and direct contents and contents needing deference as hidden, subtle, mystically opaque. Shī'ahs and Sufis, as we shall see, take up the second type vigorously and diversely. Sunnī conservatism tends to be circumspect and awed.

A working relation to this distinction argues that the plain, clear sense, if it manifestly exists, should stand without cavil and foreclose all tedious debate. Such, at any rate are many of the laws of the Qur'ān. As for the ambiguous, they may be discreetly allowed a latitude of interpretation, and even in some quarters a wide initiative, consistently with loyalty and consensus. They cannot be taken repugnantly to the clear intention of other passages. Given the very extensive use of metaphor in the Qur'ān, the pressures of circumstance and the ingenuity of Muslims, it is safe to see the relation of Scripture to community as, actually and potentially, freer and less predictable than the patterns and instincts of dogma would suggest.

Some contemporary, or near contemporary, commentary makes far-reaching appeal to the metaphorical principle and even enlarges it to involve, in a sense, the whole Quranic situation, interpreted as a seventh century parable of twentieth century concerns, needing to be "transposed," so that Muḥammad's battle against vested interest becomes an incipient socialism where the community controls the means of production; his statehood emerges as the consecration of power in the pursuit of justice; his religious leadership stands as an essential dynamism on behalf of progressive humanism. In some cases, as in that of Muḥammad Iqbāl in Indian Islam, philosophic and linguistic ingenuity comes to the aid of these reinterpretations, to find, for example, in Semitic religious terms like *Rabb* (or Lord) and *Allāh,* new connotations consistent with creative evolution and scientific views. The "ambiguity" concept then develops into a kind of foreknowing by which the Qur'ān is subsequently seen to mean what its first hearers could never have appreciated. In less able hands, this style of commentary proposes easy claims of Quranic anticipation in respect, for example, of the cutting of the Suez Canal, the invention of gunpowder, bacteriology, and the use of metallic alloys.

Such inventiveness, however, wanting to have both worlds, the dogmatic and the contemporary, has been vigorously repudiated in responsible quarters, where it is insisted that the essential message of the Qur'ān must be read in its religious character and derived from its historical setting. The argument for development, it is held, must be consistent with that double test. The crucial questions are: What did the Book mean, and intend, and achieve, in its first human context? Only when they have been loyally and rightly answered, can we properly and constructively develop its arguable relevance in a new situation. When this, the true, obedience to Surah 3:7 is given, the timeless potential of the Qur'ān may be seen to be very great indeed, as Chapter 1 above has illustrated.

But, beyond all these aspects of the Islamic Scripture lies the ultimate question: what does the holy Book mean in the inner religious experience of the loyal Muslim? It is guidance, warning, mercy, reminder, criterion, as its several titles indicate. But how does it effectuate them in his daily life? One may cite in reply its dominance in Islamic art and mosque decoration, where the sacred script receives, and in receiving confirms, a central devotion where art and the spirit combine. The chanting of the Qur'ān is, equally, the primary music of Islam. For the mosque knows no musical instruments and no choral praise. It finds its sole consecration of sound in its recital of the words of revelation. Yet, beyond calligraphy and chant, is the innermost reality by which, for the individual Muslim, the speech of God comes into the storehouse of memory and into the currency of his lips.

Memorizing and recitation, fundamental as they are to traditional Muslim piety and scholarship, are integral to ordinary believing. The Qur'ān is not simply a blueprint for society, nor only a storehouse for theology and law. It is these because it is first and always a Scripture to be confessed, and that not merely by acknowledging its status but by rehearsing its contents. Made audible in the faithful utterance of its verses, as these have been faithfully stored in the heart, it constitutes what may well be called a sacrament of mind and voice, participating in what is God's.

An approximate analogy may, at some risk, be found in the Christian sense of Holy Communion. Here is a partaking sacrament, in which bread and wine prefigure the event of "the body broken and the blood shed" and receiving them prefigures the character of faith. There is participation by the taking, in the sacramental situation of the exchange. In its different way, Quranic recital involves the heart and speech of the faithful in a taking within himself, and an expression from himself, of what he understands to be the "oracles" of God. He is faithfully doing after him what the Prophet did inclusively, for him and all Muslims, on behalf of God. This is the sense of Qur'ān, without the article, for which we were concerned at the head of this chapter. Where the New Testament speaks of "that which we have seen, and heard, and handled . . . ," Islam would speak of "that which we have heard, and remembered, and rehearsed . . . ," the appropriate "possession" of a revelation that is taken to be essentially a Book. It is by *Ḥifẓ al-Qur'ān,* as the term goes, that the Scripture is both received and known. For it seeks, not merely listeners, or hearers, or perusers, but receivers who symbolize their identity with its meanings and commands by their consecration to them of memory and tongue.

There is something abiding about this quality of things even where, as is increasingly the case, strict memorizing is no more general or entire. It may still be parabolized in the few phrases of formal prayer, including the first Surah, which figure in Arabic in all Muslim worship. These are the signs of the rest, just as the whole is, verbally, the sign of Divine communication. In the *Shahādah,* or confession, the same idea is central. Silent assent is not witness. The voice and the memory are recruited to be the tokens and the pledge of the rest of discipleship.

This answer admits, then, of a further question: what does this vocal participation in the Quranic Scripture mean in the characteristic preoccupations and emphases of the piety and faith it nurtures? The sense of the Divine authority and claim; the earnest dignity of human existence and the trivial, transitory folly of human perversity; the wistful realities of mercy and the precarious contingencies of life; the intense vividness of the eternal condition both of bliss and doom; and the impending, inescapable judgment and destiny. Relying on other areas of our study to fill out some of these, and much else in the Qur'ān, let us take a single Surah, almost at random, and ponder its emphases, its directives, its warnings, its passionate quality. For an alert reader, its own impact may be worth a tome of commentary. Choice is bewildering, yet, in a way, also unnecessary. Take Surah 25. It is Meccan, in the middle period. It bears as title one of the names of the whole, namely, "the Criterion." Let us briefly set down its contents.

> Blessed be He Who has sent down upon His servant the criterion [of truth and right] that he may warn humanity.

The Divine mention promptly excludes all associates in the Kingdom, and disowns all the idols, powerless, profitless, futile, as they are. Controversy is at once joined. The unbelievers want some extraordinary messenger, some angel, some lordling. Muḥammad is too commonplace, a forger, an upstart. But all other prophets knew these calumnies and history records the overthrow of their adversaries. So it will be again. The rejected Qur'ān is vindicated in the doom of the gainsayers.

> It shall be a Day harsh for the unbelievers. Upon that Day the evil-doer shall bite his hands and say: Would that I had walked in the way of the messenger.

The very idols, questioned in the judgment, disown their worshippers, who thus find no alibi for their misdeeds and no release from their misery.

In the living world, the signs of God abide, the measuring sun and the garment of the night, the flowing winds and the reviving showers, and after them the devastating comment that most men belie the grace in them. Each new day is a kind of resurrection. But men do not rise with it into thankfulness. "The unbeliever is always a partisan against his Lord." A brief note about the making of the creature and the angelic demur about acknowledging him is followed by the familiar, reiterated characterization of the true Muslim.

> The servants of the ever-Merciful are those who walk modestly in the earth, and who say: Peace to the ignorant when they accost them; who pass the night standing and kneeling in reverence to their Lord; and who say: Lord, ward off from us the punishment of Hell, for it is a fearful chastisement, and an evil abode and a vile resting-place; who are neither extravagant nor niggardly and observe the golden mean; who call upon no other god except God, nor slay the soul God has forbidden, except it be rightfully; who do not commit adultery, for the adulterer shall meet with evil and a double chastisement on the day of resurrection, abiding forever in disgrace, unless he repents and believes, and

does righteously. For God changes the evil doings of such into good deeds, for God is the ever-merciful, the compassionate. Whosoever repents and does rightly he turns indeed to God penitently. [The servants] are those who do not bear false witness; and when involved in profanity around them retain their honor; who when they are reminded of the signs of their Lord do not turn a blind eye and a deaf ear; who say: Lord, give us joy of our wives and children and make us examples to those who fear Thee. These will be rewarded for their patient endurance with the heavenly mansion and shall be received there with greeting and peace. They shall dwell there forever, a blessed and sure abiding place.

Here, in epitome, are the great themes of Quranic religion, and its authentic atmosphere, urgent, forceful, confident, and decisive, "a book in which there is no dubiety," holding in its reach time and eternity, angels and men, truth and error, nature and signs, the piety of the good and the doom of the evil, and all within the immediacy of a strenuous prophetic encounter with a vexing and recalcitrant people. With the final verses we are already in the themes of ethics to which we must now turn, not overlooking the sting in the closing warning to the unbelieving:

> Say: My Lord cares little that you do not call upon Him. The die is cast in that you have belied [His signs].

For this is the downrightness and the simplicity of the issue in itself.

Quranic Passages to Study

Surahs 2:1 to 37; 7:1 to 36; 11:1 to 66; Surahs 21; 32; 35; 50; 55; 57; and 87.

Some Questions

1. What is the relation between the Islamic Scripture and the Arabic lan guage?
2. What does recitation of the Qur'ān mean in religious experience?
3. What, in broad terms, are the basic Quranic themes?
4. How does the Qur'ān fit into the pattern it affirms of a continuity of revelation through all the prophets?
5. Does the Qur'ān *need* to be rearranged chronologically?

4.
Law

"A transcendence rigged up to slander mortal existence" was Nietzsche's verdict on Christianity. He proposed "a radical counter-doctrine," to denounce theistic moralism as a libel on life, and to restore human living to its due hilarity and liberty.[1] The esthetical, he insisted, had to displace the ethical, as the only concern of man. God himself was a reckless artist, reflecting His own tensions in a lawless creating and destroying, a great jester for ever doing and undoing himself.

Islam, had Nietzsche known it, must surely have incurred the same condemnation as Christianity. Beyond their many divergencies, the two faiths are one in their conviction of man as under ethical authority, as a citizen of a cosmic order, ruled by a Divine rectitude, by a God of justice who wills the law of the good and the true within which life belongs and to which its mortality returns.

There is, indeed, no more complete ethical theism than Islam. Its genius, we often find it said, is law rather than theology. The point is well made. But it would be truer to say that its strength lies in theology as law. It understands the world and man as set under God, constituted by creation, guided by revelation and summoned to submission. Awareness of God is, therefore, primarily awareness of obligation and accountability. Just as the law from Sinai set Jewry under the claims of the Divine Lordship within what they understood as sacred history, so the Divine law in Islam makes all life and activity the realm of God's authority and man's obedience. The knowledge Islam enjoys in the revelation has to do directly with the demands of God and only indirectly with His nature. Law, we may say, is religion and religion is law.

The general term embracing both is *Sharī'ah,* or "way," or right path of action, both ritual and ethical. This is the Torah of Islam, received through the Prophet and elaborated in the first three centuries of Islam through the gathering experience of Muslims in its custody. Law is often denoted by a term earlier than *Sharī'ah,* namely *Fiqh,* or "understanding." The *fuqahā',* or "legists," were the men of discernment who drew out, for actual jurisprudence, or life-direction and due order, the implications of the Divine will. The word *Fiqh* combines the twin ideas of directive and response, of God in command and man in surrender.

Total and inclusive as it is, this *islām,* or law-abidingness, of man within the structure of Divine direction is not properly seen as passive or servile. It belongs with the dignity of man as entrusted with the dominion (*khilāfah*) of the world, and as undertaking the *amānah,* or trust, of suzerainty under God. (See Surahs 2:30 and 33:72). The earth is the Lord's and not man's. But the 'empire' over it is given into man's hands and presupposes capacities of intelligence and freedom, as well as of loyalty. In that responsibility to God with and for the world, lies the issue of man's being.

The intelligent nature of man's *Fiqh,* or conformity to the Divine will, does not mean that the *Sharī'ah* is derived from rationality. On the contrary, it is given by God and has no other ground. Even where its contents take their definition from sources other than the Qur'ān and tradition, they possess, nevertheless, the same revelatory and mandatory quality. The *Sharī'ah* is what God commands and what men obey. The very legalism it may engender is, arguably, a lesser evil than the reduction of its imperative force. Submission is tested, exemplified, made concrete, even in exacting rituals and matters that reason may find pointless. One can more wholly register Divine demand by discerning no other point, of utility or arguability, in what it enjoins. The spirit that complains against the letter may soon have no more context in which either to complain or to attain. That debate, of course, continues—and not only in Islam.

In this way Muslims see in the *Sharī'ah* an all-embracing sacred law, the source of which is God's will and the motive obedience to Him. Its content is understood, classically, as governing and determining all areas of life—personal, communal, social, civil, political, and cultic. The strictly ritual and devotional provisions are the sacramental *foci* of what is throughout religious, in the sense that it is God-aware, God-responsive and God-ordained. One does not rightly speak of religion *and* morality, of morality *and* law: they are identical—though the problems implicit in seeing them so are serious and lively. There is a sense in which one can only equate law and life, religion and existence by neglecting either the ideals of the one or the realities of the other. But the hope of their identity is magnificent, provided we are alert to its perpetual frustration. There lies the whole inner tension of Islamic law and ethics.

The Godward relation of men, in this exceptionless quality, was, from the earliest centuries, understood as threefold. Things to be believed are given in *Īmān,* or faith. It is the obligation of man to receive and confess them. Things to be done in rite and ordinance are given in *Dīn,* or religion. It is the duty of man to perform and do them. Things commanded as good and vetoed as evil are also given, in what Arabic calls: *Al-Amr bi-l-Ma'rūf* and *Al-Nahī 'ān al-Munkar.* It is the obligation of man to fulfill the one and abjure the other. In the whole *Sharī'ah* are the gathered prescriptions and regulations legislating for the whole complex range of human affairs and relationships.[2] By all these the innate calling, freedom, and stature of man, in body and soul, in family and society, in order and well-being, are to find their realization. Within the whole there are wide stretches of moral option or neutrality, where the *Sharī'ah* does not tediously enjoin, but yet hallows and conditions the choices and works of Muslim mankind.

The articles of faith, or *Īmān,* are God and His unity, the books, the prophets and messengers of God, angels as bearers of God's commands and revelation, the last day and judgment, and the Divine decree of good and evil, that is, the Divine criteria or determination, of reality and of destiny. There have been endless debates on these themes, not least the last, and a diversity of emphases and interpretation. But broadly they constitute the dogmatic structure of Islam, set the doctrinal texture of Muslim thought and give the house of Islam its characteristic temper of soul. It was the intention of our first three chapters to indicate their main significance and their historical genesis in seventh century Arabia.

The faith acceptance of the right Muslim, however, is summed up and articulated in the briefer *Shahādah,* or confession, prefaced by the singular: *"I* bear witness. . ."

To say: "There is no god but God and Muhammad is the *Rasūl* of God" is the first of the five articles, or "pillars," of *Dīn* and joins both faith and practice. Its personal, vocal avowal is the criterion of being Muslim, though from time to time inconsistency of conduct led purists to insist that it had to be corroborated by fidelity of life. Neglect of the rest of the *Sharī'ah* disqualified *Shahādah* also. At the crux of this issue was the range of *Niyyah,* or "intention," by which a valid confession had to be made. Three other pillars of religion, namely *Ṣalāt, Ṣaum,* and *Ḥajj,* prayer, fast and pilgrimage, respectively, will be discussed in the next chapter. They belong under Law but may be studied as Liturgy.

The remaining pillar is *Zakāt,* or almsgiving—an institution which undergirds a whole philosophy of social responsibility in Islam. From a very early point, allegiance involved obligation to fellow Muslims who were poor or victimized. The help of the Medinan converts to the Meccan emigrés became an abiding theme of tradition and example. The needs of the original and growing community were for solidarity, mutuality, interdependence, and resources for propagation, as well as the sealing of accessions. All these, as the phrase went, were "in the way of God." *Zakāt* was thus the cement of Islam, always joined with prayer in the double Quranic phrase: "Perform the *Ṣalāt* and bring the *Zakāt,"* and willful withholding of it a sign of rebellion. The *jizyah,* or tax on non-Muslim minorities surviving under Islam was always carefully distinguished from *Zakāt,* thus further enforcing its communal character. Both the paying and the disbursing signalized participation in the household of the faith.

"Lend to God a good loan" says Surah 73:20. *Zakāt* is understood as a means to repentance and atonement, as a way of practical reconciliation, and as a parable of brotherliness. It also symbolizes those voluntary acts of generosity that season common life. As a tradition says: "A camel lent out for milk is alms, good works are alms, your smile to your neighbor is alms." These deeds, sometimes called *Ṣadaqāt,* to distinguish them from legal alms (though the term is not consistently held to that sense), should not, however, excuse the doer from *Zakāt* proper. The obligatory cannot rightly be displaced by the voluntary. Nor, in the eyes of literalists, can *Zakāt* be equated with state taxation for social welfare purposes, since then the element of obligatoriness is not of the *Sharī'ah,* but of the fiscal authority of the state. For most modern thinkers, nevertheless, the ideology arguable from this pillar of religion, namely an active social conscience, is regarded as achieved, under the different conditions of the modern world, by the sanctions of state action. The organization of the mosque and of the religious leadership cannot feasibly cope with the task of collecting and disbursing even a modest poor relief in the teeming, complex world of this century. It is surely not an un-Islamic doctrine that what is enjoined by religion can be organized and implemented by the political power.

At all events the intelligent enunciation of *Zakāt* today makes the case for socialist economy. The root meaning of the term is "to purify." Surah 9:103 says: "Take of their wealth an offering [*ṣadaqah*] to purify them and cleanse [*tuzakkihim*] them thereby." The doctrine is that property is validated as a private right and enjoyment, provided a portion of it is devoted to the common need, in token of the corporate awareness that should characterize all personal possession. This paid portion "purifies," that is, legitimatizes, what is retained. Without this active conscience, retention and ownership would be impure and disqualified. The community has not only a stake in, but also a claim on, the individual's *amwāl* or substance. It is easy to see a direct line of argument from this central thesis of the faith to the Marxist doctrine of the labor theory of value, of the community as the source and context of all worth, and of a communal ownership of what is vital to common life. The last theme, however, must be subject to the implicit approval of ownership, once socially conscious, which is involved in the whole ordinance of *Zakāt.* The abolition of private ownership would terminate the feasibility of the pillar of *Dīn;* and that, argue the orthodox theorists, could never be the intention of God.

Clearly, there is room for wide divergence of view here about the mutual bearings of Islamic alms and ideologies of wealth and of communism. There were, likewise, through the centuries, many varieties of interpretation on the practical aspects of *Zakāt,* the proportions of income payable and their variation according to the kind of income involved. Intricate as these are, they have little bearing on the religious dimension. Agricultural *Zakāt,* wrote Al-Fīrūzābādī,

> . . . is only obligatory on cereals eaten for food and cultivated by men, such as wheat, barley, millet, sorghum, rice and the like: then it applies to vegetables such as lentils, chickpeas, vetches, beans, and peas. Fruits are not subject, except for dates and grapes, to which Al-Shāfi'ī used to add olives, turmeric, and saffron . . . The taxable minimum, when the grain has been threshed and the fruit

dried is five camel burdens, for sixteen hundred Baghdad *ruṭls,* but for rice . . . the minimum is ten camel burdens.[3]

We leave the threshing-floor and the weighing-shed, the tax-gatherers and the peasants, to return to them and their whole society, in another guise. The specific pillars of *Dīn* uphold the house of Muslim conduct and character as the *Sharī'ah* enjoins them. The Qur'ān, as we saw in the quotation in Chapter 3 from Surah 25, mingles general ethics with particular commands and prohibitions. Our exposition had better seek to study first the right moral "manner" of the true Muslim, and then the explicit legal provisions. The whole, however, needs to be prefaced by some reference to the sources of Islamic law and ethical ideal.

Given the Qur'ān and the tradition, the notion of such a need may seem, at first sight, perplexing. Is not the sacred Scripture a sufficient source in itself, as amplified by the *Sunnah,* or example of Muḥammad, already reviewed? The answer, plainly, is No. The Qur'ān is complete as a criterion, as the test of repugnancy. But it antedated many themes and issues encountered by Islam in its expansion. It relates to a setting which, limited and circumscribed in time and place, could not afford the precedents and directives demanded by an unlimited future. Even within its own scene, there were matters on which it was silent. There had, then, to be a superstructure of law, built upon it. The large growth of tradition to supplement it is evidence enough of this necessity and of its legitimacy. As a second source of guidance, tradition, or *Hadīth,* draws its authority from the general exemplariness and inspiration of Muḥammad as distinct from his Quranic role proper. The status of the revelatory instrument sanctions an enlargement of the law. The dead yet speaketh.

Yet together, these two still do not suffice. Sunnī Islam relies upon two further sources. One is *Qiyās,* or analogy. By this, the legists argued from the intention of some specific rule of Qur'ān or *Sunnah,* to cover some matter, arguable from, though not stated in, the original. The compulsory recording of commercial transactions to prevent fraud might be said to cover, by analogy, the registration of marriages, where in fact a far more serious transaction of trust is involved. Such extension might well be resisted on other grounds and the debate over legitimate analogical extension of the *Sharī'ah* was often profuse and divisive. But the principle, and that of *ra'y,* or opinion, with which it was linked, was a useful means of law affirming.

There were, however, pressures of necessity which could in no way be satisfied in these terms. Recourse was had, therefore, to a fourth and much ampler source of law, namely *Ijmā',* or consensus. Founded on the conviction that the community as such would not long, or finally, "converge on an error," *Ijmā'* in effect entrusted the enlargement of law to the collective fidelity. Innovation—a concept always close to heresy in Islam—would be saved from excess, from pretension, from distortion, if it commended itself, in the long run, to the whole household of the faith. Here seemed to be a sure principle of development which would be secure against the vagaries of individualists and the deviations of the sectaries. Was there not safeguard in numbers? Had the Prophet not agreed that after the Qur'ān and his example the community would be the proper referee? Where else in fact could faith custody turn, if not to the faith custodians, the believers incorporate? Is not this principle, in some measure, universal through all religions, at least those which do not retreat into the mystical and the exotic?

Thus matters of new, or newly interpreted, law were to be authenticated by the agreement of the common mind, always, of course, consistently with the other primary sources. Yet *Sharī'ah* so derived had no less sacred and binding a character.

But consensus does not just emerge. It needs pioneers. It requires opinion initiators, before its mind can be formed. This means the kindred institution of *Ijtihād,* or endeavor, initiative, from which potential *Ijmā'* can arise and by which it may be stimulated. *Ijtihād,* however, needed to be hedged with provisos and prerequisites. It was not open to any and every "lay" Muslim to pretend to it, but demanded expert knowledge of the Qur'ān, skills of grammar, and subleties of legal acumen, beyond the range of the average believer. Every system begets its pundits—in the case of Islam the shaikhs, the *fuqahā'* and the *'ulamā',* qualified to venture, with proper circumspection, the initiatives which might, in turn, merit general acceptance.

To these themes belongs the deep cleavage between Sunnis and Shī'ahs which we postpone to our study of the *Ummah* below. Meanwhile, it suffices to note that Shī'ahs disavowed *Ijmā',* relying on their Imāms to "guarantee" Islamic truth. In a different sense from Sunnis, they exalted *Ijtihād* but located it even more stringently in their "spiritual guides," understood as speaking in the name and by the light of the Hidden Imām. Their authority, exempt from the need for *Ijmā',* was the more assertive.

Among Sunnis there was no clear or final dictum as to the area or period within which consensus could be said to be assured, nor as to the precise means of ascertaining it. But the basic idea of *Ijmā'* set the elaboration of *Sharī'ah* squarely within the community, and this was both its strength and its wisdom. Four Sunnī schools of law developed between the eighth and ninth centuries and differed widely in the details of their teaching, namely the Ḥanafī, the Mālikī, the Shāfi'ī, and the Ḥanbalī. The last was the most strict and uncompromising. Every Sunnī Muslim belongs to one or other school, and they are distributed unevenly throughout the whole Islamic world.

Between the schools there were debates about the limits and safeguards of *Ijmā'* and of *ra'y,* and over the powers and credentials of the masters of *Ijtihād*. The most crucial of these controversies concerned the question whether at any time enlargement of law by *Ijmā'* could be said to be complete so that the "door" of *Ijtihād* must be said to be closed. This issue became the main ground of contention between those wanting a static, secure situation, immune from change, and those who sensed the necessity of growth and flexibility. The problem, of course, has been overtaken in modern times by the sheer pressures of irresistible change, requiring not merely an open door but levelled walls. But by the same token the bewilderments of loyalty are the more intense. Yet, even now, the concept of consensus remains both a stay and a solace. For, in the last analysis, it entrusts the continuity of *Sharī'ah* to a living trusteeship, by dint of which it may hope to ensure a living perpetuation.

There were different ways, in medieval times, of assessing the how and where, the whence and whither, of a communal mind. Three ideas, in particular, emerged by the third Muslim century, namely *Istiḥsān,* or what impressed with an intrinsic rightness as "good," *Istiṣlāḥ,* or what seemed in the public interest as beneficial, and *Istiṣḥāb,* or what had good commendation or associations. These the *fuqahā'* sought either to enlarge or to restrain, according to their instinct for enterprise or conservation. They could be used either to instigate or to curb development, as mood or need dictated. The whole concept of consensus had only the scantiest of direct Quranic ground as far as specific reference is concerned. But it certainly coincided with a deep conviction of solidarity resulting from faith and conformity, a solidarity which could, therefore, in turn attest and discriminate what faith and conformity should entail. It stands, then, as a most characteristic institution of Islam and serves to illustrate a vital principle of religion everywhere—the interreliance of belonging and behaving. It formalizes and regulates what we may perhaps loosely call the compatibility of change.

Even before *Ijmā'* and *Ijtihād* were juridically defined and established, the physical enlargement of Islam had brought about a widening and broadening of its scope of law and practice, simply by the rapid and diversified recruitment of new peoples and cultures. This occurred, in large measure, through contribution of customary law, or *'urf,* as found within the conquered lands, to the *corpus* of the *Sharī'ah.* Conditional on compatibility with the Qur'ān and the *Sunnah,* large areas of local law and custom came, with their peoples, into the fold of Muslim *fiqh.* This generous tolerance of the familiar worlds of new Muslims may be seen, in part, as an application of the clue within *Ijmā',* though much of it happened willy-nilly and without formal auspices. In the first centuries, the fertility of tradition, as studied in Chapter 2, enabled incoming habits and values and practice to find validity and allowance under the authority of Muḥammad's actual or supposed example. This sanction for customary law through the tradition of the Prophet became less feasible with the passage of time and greater remoteness from the Hijāz. But the pattern of hospitality has remained and goes far to account for the ready adoption of Islam, not least in Africa. Yet, whatever the compromises thus incurred, they were effectively subdued to the basic identity of the *Sharī'ah*-people, and there was a resilience in the *Sharī'ah* itself against debasement. In the acceptance of *'urf* into *Sharī'ah,* Islam, in the main, was able to allow a gradualism which did not require entire transition in one generation. Meanwhile, the tests of a worthy Islam remained intact, in Qur'ān, *Sunnah,* and community. There were, moreover, plenty of means to their enforcement, for example, in those intriguing officers of Islamic *Sharī'ah,* the *muḥtasib,* or custodian of morals and inspector of trade, and the *mutawwiʿ* "the maker-obedient."

To take due stock of the worthy Muslim it is perhaps best to set down here the Quranic passage most resembling a single code and to review, in sequel to it, the major themes of Islamic ethical concern, both of injunction and prohibition, and the more important items of personal law. The passage is in Surah 17, from verses 22 to 39.

> Do not set up another god with God, lest you find yourself in shame and desolation. Your Lord has commanded that you serve none save Him. Show kindness to parents, whether one or both of them attains old age with you. Do not be round or impatient with either of them, but speak kindly words to them. Lower to them the wing of humility tenderly and say: My Lord, have mercy on them, as they nurtured me when I was little. Your Lord knows well what is in your hearts, if you be true of soul. He is all forgiving to those who seek Him.
>
> Give to the kinsman his due and to the needy and the wayfarer, and do not squander your substance, for squanderers are brothers to Satan. Satan is ever thankless to his Lord. And if you turn from them, anticipating the wherewithal from your Lord's mercy, then at least speak to the needy kindly.
>
> Do not have your hand chained to your neck; yet do not be open-handed to utter excess, or you will end up with reproach and bankruptcy.
>
> Your Lord gives with bountiful hand and with sparing hand to whom He wills. Truly He knows and observes His servants.
>
> Do not kill your children for fear of poverty. We will provide both for you and for them. To kill them is a most grievous sin.
>
> Come not near to adultery, which is foul and an evil way. Do not kill any man—a deed God forbids, except for rightful cause. If a man is slain unjustly, We have appointed to next of kin the right to satisfaction. But let him not carry his vengeance beyond the due, for there is counter retaliation.
>
> Handle the property of the orphan in all integrity, until he comes of age. Keep your bond, for you are accountable.
>
> Give full measure when you measure, and weigh with just scales. That is better and fairer in the end.
>
> Do not pursue things you have no knowledge of. Hearing, sight and heart—all these faculties of a man will be held responsible.
>
> Do not strut proudly on the earth. You cannot cleave the earth or match the mountains in stature. All such ways are evil with your Lord.
>
> All this is given you by revelation of the wisdom of your Lord, and set not up any other god beside God.

There is, here, a close resemblance to the Decalogue (without the Sabbath provision): anti-idolatry, care and honor of parents, prohibition of infanticide, and of murder outside legitimate vengeance, prohibition of adultery, integrity with property and trade and with rights of orphans. Interspersed with the commands, positive and negative, are directives about attitudes and character, particularly kindliness, integrity and humility.

The traditional ethics of Islam divide conduct, inward and outward, into five categories—things enjoined, things commended, things deplored, things prohibited, and a central area where actions fall into none of the other four categories and may thus be said to be "neutral," though they are not outside the Divine watchfulness or the human responsibility and may readily merge or tend into one of the other categories. There is the severest condemnation for the omission of the obligatory or the committing of the forbidden, and relative censure for the neglect of the desirable or indulgence in the deplored.

The Muslim scheme is readily capable of universality, in that it does not relate contractually to the acquisition of any particular territory, nor is it vested in a private account of history. Its provisions, nevertheless, reflect the time and the economy of its origins. Retaliation is proper, but not beyond due limits. Like the Biblical law of requital, it is concerned with *one* man for a man, not ten. There is throughout a deep, practical note of "what is better in the end," and an underlying sense of common finitude and frailty, of the perennial rightness of "tenderness," and an urgent sense of the final Divine accounting.

The Qur'ān, in several other passages, echoes and enforces these injunctions and qualities, and tradition multiplies their exemplification in the Prophet and the companions. Humanity under Islam is gathered with these prototypes into a sort of corporate responsibility over good and evil. The right and the wrong behavior is not a take-it-or-leave-it individualism. The body communal is there to care for right conduct among all. The very term *Ma'rūf,* noted above, meaning "the good," has the primary sense of "the known," the acknowledged, while evil is *al-munkar,* the (corporately) disowned. Good and evil have their sole definition in the Divine authority, but the care for their recognition lies with the house of Islam. The spiritual resources of this care lie in the conscience and moral health of the whole body of Muslim humanity and in their sense of encounter awaiting in the world to come. Its verdict in debatable issues could take shape in the *fatwas,* or legal opinions, given by the *muftis* within the authority of *Ijmā'* and in exegesis, for the guidance of the faithful.

The character of Islamic law is most readily illustrated in the realm of personal status and matters of marriage, divorce, and inheritance. It was here that the Qur'ān itself was most specific, whereas in other areas of legislation, such as matters of administration and civil jurisprudence it was relatively silent in detail.

Marriage in Islam is a simple contractual relationship or agreement, verbally exchanged between the two parties in the presence of witnesses. It has no sacramental status or quality of "one flesh" in the Christian sense of the "estate" of matrimony. The Muslim bride says simply: "I marry you to myself," and the bridegroom says: "I accept your marriage to me." Sexual relationships outside marriage, except in the case of slavery, are prohibited. The rights of the bride require that due status, contract and provision, be assured, before sexuality can legitimately be taken.

It is important to emphasize this essential dignity of the married state. For while Islam does not give to marriage a status incapable of concurrent duplication, the Qur'ān nevertheless comes very close in certain passages, to a view of the wedded state that sets it among the "signs of God," that ought properly to lead into reverent gratitude and hallowedness. The most notable passage is Surah 30:21: "And of His signs is that He created for you, of yourselves, wives, that you might live in joy with them, and He ordained between you love and mercy."

The benediction of the gift of sex in marriage, however, does not necessarily argue monogamy. Provided each wife has her just rights, the *Sharī'ah* allows up to four wives. The context of this permission needs to be carefully noted in Surah 4:3. For, though it has been taken by the traditional practice for centuries as positive allowance of plurality within the limit of four, the verse makes this hinge on a proviso which, in the view of many today, is unattainable and amounts, therefore, to a virtual prohibition.

In the first place, the whole matter is within the theme of provision for orphans and seems to assume the widowhood ensuing from early warfare. The authority to marry "two, three, or four," if it seems good, is conditioned by the proviso: "If you fear you will not deal equally, then marry only one," or the female slaves. That operative phrase may mean feasible equalities—economic support and rotation of sexual intercourse (a matter that traditions strongly enjoin so that no wife is left forlorn), or it may arguably mean a quite impracticable equality of emotional affection and delight. If the latter interpretation is followed (which a few other passages about the impossiblity of "equality" seem to hint), then there is, in fact, no provision at all for plurality. The condition being unattainable, the permission lapses.

From a sacramental perspective about marriage we are still left with the question whether a "virtual" prohibition is appropriate. Will not the notion of duplicate marriage *ipso facto* constitute an unwarrantable injustice to an existing wife, since the self cannot be wholly given save wholly? But Islamic *Sharī'ah* holds that there is no inherent wrong in plurality, and it may be noted that the "fear" referred to in Surah 4:3 can only be proven after the plural marriages exist. The man who feels a confidence can, within this authority, go ahead and his failure to be equal, if it occurs, will be subsequent to the fact.

In current practice this deterring exegesis is more and more widely relied on to sustain single marriage, and in most Muslim societies today even dual, not to speak of threefold or fourfold, marriages are increasingly disallowed. By the same token the abiding Quranic sense of the contractual dignity of sex is reinforced and comes close to the logic that monogamy is its most valid expression. Economic and social factors tend in the same direction. Nevertheless, despite the specific changes in the *Sharī'ah* law of many countries, there are voices sustaining the old exegesis and the former pluralism as more appropriate to the physiological nature of men, more compassionate towards women and more loyal to our liberties under God. Throughout these assessments, however, it is well to keep always in view the *Sharī'ah*'s reprobation of adultery and extramarital intercourse, since this belongs powerfully with its positive and vigilant concept of marriage. There is in traditional Muslim mores an alert jealousy about the sanctity of women's honor and of the duties that belong with men's rights in women.

It is in this context that the provisions about divorce should be set. Traditionally, divorce is possible at the man's will simply by his declaration of it. Inasmuch as it may be followed by reconciliation, up to a third repetition, it has tended to be a safety valve for hasty enmities. Only after a third divorce does a wife cease to be available for remarriage to her husband, though even then she may again become so after an interim marriage to another party. When divorce occurs, according to the *Sharī'ah,* the wife must be freely let go, after the stipulated period to avoid confusion about paternity, and not distrained or exploited. There were several particulars in which Islam brought improvement into the lot of Arab women, and in Khadījah, Muḥammad's first wife, Fāṭimah his daughter and wife of 'Alī, and other women, it has ensured a strong female element in its heritage of example. There are large grounds for seeing Islam as constituting, in sundry particulars, "a man's world." But its understanding of "the stronger sex" (Surah 4:34) is tempered by the deep sense of mutuality and the tribute of contractuality, tragically as the contract of marriage often worked out in the fashion of the ḥarīm and the patterns of *The Arabian Nights.*

The Prophet's own marriages, eleven in all, were exceptional in their dynastic concern, in the heirlessness that dogged him, and in the diplomatic and political necessities of his recovery of Mecca. The pattern of his single marriage to Khadījah while she lived is cited as no less relevant than the later situation, where, in fact, almost all Muḥammad's added wives were widows, or divorced.

In matters of inheritance, women normally receive one half of the male share for equivalent relationship, in blood kinship or marital connection.

In the brevity of our discussion of personal status there has been a merging of past and present views. The question is, therefore, implicit about the actual status of the *Sharī'ah* when revision occurs. The specific situation in personal status law in the several Muslim states is too complex and diverse for the barest exposition here. In many, plural marriage is precluded and divorce sharply curtailed. In some, notably Egypt and Tunisia, the *Shar'ī* Courts that formerly administered the religious law have been abolished. In Turkey since the nineteen-twenties there has been an avowedly secular pattern of social legislation based on western models and deliberately repudiating both the source and sanction of the old order. But though abandoned or eroded, the *Sharī'ah* concept may still be retrieved in reinterpretation. There is the argument that in its essential dynamism Islam is conserved, not depleted, by such changes. They may be claimed as within the evolving intention of the sacred and in some cases, as in that of single marriage, the gist can be credibly read from, or into, the revealed Scripture. It is possible to digest a wide measure of modern reform, even to the apparent disqualification of centuries of supposedly authentic usage, and still derive it, through a broad appeal to *Ijmā',* from the orthodox heritage.

Such advocacy, however, by the same token, merits and incurs the strictures and rebuttals that an anxious conservatism inspires. Though seldom outwardly successful, these voices have to be respected. For they represent a form of fidelity for which modernity is a menace. The very fact that they hold for an Islam against the odds is a measure of their integrity in it. But the more clearly they see what they *should* be, the more remote they are from being it effectively. There is an easier task for those who align their Islam with the world, than for those who would conform their world to Islam.

Yet, in either case, and through all the varieties between, it is feasible to claim that the end and essence is the Divine authority over loyal people. What then of that final question, returning whence we started? God-aware, God-responsive, God-ordained—is this a viable pattern of law and how is it sustained in the postures of worship? The latter is a theme which takes us into Chapter 5. The former will always be involved in the alternative of human autonomy. But is it really an alternative except as idolatrous? Islam believes men receive the substance of such autonomy only in turning back from its pretension. It sees the values and meanings we experience within ourselves as truly grounded in a Lordship at once absolute and compassionate.

It is the idols that are the conspiracy of transcendence against man. They are disarmed and disowned, not by a secular competition with them, but by a true submission. The "counterdoctrine" which exposes their tyranny and breaks their power is, simply, "God is greater." Islam sees law under God as the true education of man. If religion may be said to be "reading the text of the universe in the original," Islam finds it written in the imperative. And so its worship is erect and prostrate, and then again erect.

Quranic Passages to Study

Surah 2:168 to 177, 215 to 245 and 262 to the end.

Surah 4:1 to 70.

Surahs 16:89 to 99; 24:20 to 34; 31:12 to 19; 33:28 to 35; 49:11 to 14; and Surah 65.

Some Questions

1. What are the sources of law in Islam and how are they interrelated?

2. Explain the concept of *Zakāt* and its significance for social responsibility and for the criticism of economic systems in Islam.

3. How has traditional Islam understood and ordered the institution of marriage?

4. What emphases in respect to character and conduct are to be found in Islamic *Sharīʿah?*

5. Why is it that the most characteristic activity of Islamic scholarship has to do with the interpretation and study of law?

6. What, in your view, are the problems of a theologically based ethics, as Islam exemplifies them?

5.
Liturgy

All religious ritual, according to Immanuel Kant, was "pious playing"—*Frommes Spielwerk* he called it, adding that the only valid way to worship God was by moral states of mind. To imagine one could do so by words and ceremony was an idle fancy, a piece of superstitious play-acting.

The great philosopher did not know Muslims at prayer, since there were no mosques in Konigsberg, where his days were spent. Had he known them even his rational disapproval might have wavered, or paused to reconsider. For nowhere is there a simpler worship or a more direct ritual. Nowhere is there a religious devotion less calculated than that of Islam to deceive itself about its own significance.

Certainly there is nothing "playful" about the piety of the mosque. "God," says the Qur'ān, "did not create the world in jest." (Surahs 21:16 and 44:38). On that conviction the prayers of Islam rest. There could hardly be a more formal simplicity. There is no priesthood, no bewildering incantation, no solemn music, no curtained mysteries, no garments for sacred wear contrasted with those of the street and of the marketplace. All proceeds within a congregational unison in which the *imām,* or leader, does no more than occupy the space before the niche and set the time for the sequence of movements in which all participate. The essential sacrament, for such it is, is within each person's own privacy, requiring as it does the use of his own limbs and lips. Since all move in rhythm of posture and with identical words, the experience incorporates each individual into a communal whole. No one is spectator of "official" acts. No one is obliged to delegate his own intention to another's action, or liable to annul his physical presence, through inaction, into an absence of mind. The mechanical or the repetitive, which are anyhow unavoidable in all recurrent worship, are such as still to engage each with all and all with each, without distinction of value, function or act, while reducing none to passivity.

Before taking this further we had better first justify the word "Liturgy" as the proper title for this chapter. It might, at first glance, seem ill-chosen. It is not a normal usage in this context and could stand for features of ritual quite uncongenial to Islam. The root idea, however, is deeply apposite. "Liturgy" in origin means acts of public spirit on the part of private people, gifts in prizes for athletic games, or underwriting the music and arts of the community: the *leitourgia* of the Greeks. It passed thence into Christian currency to describe the acts of personal surrender in the setting of the celebration of the passion of Christ in holy communion or participation, and thence into religious usage as denoting those exchanges of discipleship with Lordship that sacraments embody, always in a social context.

Islam, as we know, has no paradigmatic events for celebration, no Passover because no Exodus, no Lord's Supper because no Cross. Qur'ān-recitation is the nearest equivalent to being "baptized into Moses," or sharing "in the night in which Jesus was betrayed." For it puts into faithful mouths the very utterance that speaks from heaven. This is clearly a personal activity which needs no formal figuration, no ordered ceremonial, but only a private learning and reciting. But there is the same dutifulness, the same corporate context, the same social implication, and these make "liturgy" the right term to borrow. There are the same threefold elements of Godward duty, personal obligation, and collective response. The Arabic word *Dīn*—things *done* in Islam as distinct from *Īmān,* or things *believed,* and usually translated "religion" or "religious acts"—is very near to this broad nature of liturgy.

For prayer, *Ṣalāt,* is definitely a deed. "Perform—establish—the prayer" is the formula. So it is with all the five pillars of *Dīn* on which *Dār al-Islām* is built, namely Witness, Prayer, Alms, Fasting, and Pilgrimage. Their form and content must be studied as the intensive religious dimension, the duties of Islamic identity *per se.*

"Intensive" is the right word, inasmuch as being Muslim is properly to be diffused through all the areas of life and not located in specifically ritual acts. The "extensive" character of Islam, its insistent refusal to isolate religion from the rest of existence, must control the interpretation of the things that are, nonetheless, specifically "religious." The implied paradox here is, of course, inescapable. One cannot enjoin, or even identify, what is only diffused: its very vagueness would be its undoing. Islam is in no mind to exhort to godfearingness and give the exhortation no ritual focus or particular duties. Muslims must stand, and bow, and prostrate, observe a daily fast between the seasons of one moon, pay dues to God, and go on pilgrimage. But these necessary expressions of loyalty are to be taken as the tokens of an inclusive and active sense of God which is more than they.—

So, then, to ablution the washing, known as *wuḍū',* which prefaces the prayer. Is this conceivably a kind of self-baptism? From one angle, certainly, No. For it is self-administered, as baptism can never be. Moreover, it is recurrent and has no twice-born, or transcendent, implication. In a different sense, however, Yes. For it is the only formal cleansing in Islam and makes ready the way to the Lord. Mosques and water belong together, where water can be had. Prayer is readiest beside a spring, or well, or pool, and requires for its preparation the simplest of bodily routines. The ritual purity that washing serves is within a private competence. The self does what the self needs and is aware of itself in the doing, and the action moves with the movement of life. There is broadly in Islam no inclusive crisis about sin, only a habitual transaction about sins. The washing of the body serves a sort of hygiene of the self. We approach God through a symbol of purification that demands neither subtlety nor passion. It neither beats its breast nor rends its garments. It prosaically washes hands and arms and face and ankles, and proceeds into the act of *Ṣalāt.*

The daily rites of prayer (*Ṣalāt*) are five in number and consist of between two and five sequences of movement and liturgical recitation. The varying number depends upon the time of day, but each sequence contains the same pattern beginning and ending in the erect posture and including bowing and prostrating. The final sequence of each time of prayer concludes with a salutation to right and left upon all the people of Islam. It is a liturgy of adoration and submission, affirming the unity, sovereignty, and greatness of God.

The surest way into its nature is through the *Fātiḥah,* which it embodies. This is the opening Chapter of the Qur'ān, which runs:

> In the Name of God, the merciful Lord of mercy.
> Praise be to God, the Lord of all being,
> The merciful Lord of mercy,
> Master of the Day of Judgement.
> Thee alone we serve and to Thee alone we come for aid.
> Guide us in the straight path,
> The path of those whom Thou hast blessed,
> Not of those against whom there is displeasure,
> Nor of those who go astray.

These words are the heart of Muslim devotion, the only terms in which *Ṣalāt* is ever petitionary. "Guide us in the straight path," the way of the *Sunnah* in the *Ummah,* the doing of the works of *Dīn* and the keeping of the truths of *Īmān,* in contrast with the ways of the devious and willful under the Divine displeasure. This note of distinctiveness in Islam is inseparable from its nature. It is the final faith and its people the community of a "universal election" of favor, by dint of the saving sign of right guidance. No mention of "the fathers" here: the operative pronoun *al-ladhīna,* "those . . . ," incorporates the dead, the living, and the unborn, yet not by any ethnic test, nor in some certainty of blood relationship, but only in the mercy of God, whose counsels are its own and upon which neither race nor esteem may presume. It is the company of "the doers of the will" of God, but it is not within the will of the doers to ensure a claim. Hence the force of the petition: "guide us *in* the straight path." The fact of the Qur'ān already brings us *to* the path. The *Fātiḥah* is a prayer for conformity and acceptability within it. All this stands on the emphatic protestation: "Thee it is we worship; Thee it is we seek unto for aid." Prayer is only true where it explicitly disowns all other recourse, or resource. For our singular dependence is the effective meaning of the unity of God. No *Shirk* here: no "practice" of any other presence, no deviation to an idol for comfort or for succor. To harbor a superstitious soul is not truly to pray. The sanctuary is where the theist may be least consistent. Hence the insistent cry: "*Thee* it is we worship."

The plural there is instinctive. While the confession: "I bear witness that there is no god but God; Muḥammad is the apostle of God," is in the singular, the *Fātiḥah* throughout has plural human pronouns. Yet the *Ṣalāt* need not be congregational save at noon on Friday. Where mosques are accessible they are to be preferred, and especially so in Ramaḍān. But a mosque in the last resort is not a building: it is a place of prostration and any patch of ground in ritual purity suffices where a human frame may stretch itself—a fact about Islam which accounts in large measure for the naturalness of its occasions and the contagion in its expansion. A faith that does not need to house its worshippers has no walls to hide its creed.

The mosque sermon is mainly and by tradition an exercise in exhortation, rather than an exposition of belief. Set between the call to prayer and the full *Ṣalāt,* it is more an expression of the solidarity, than the justification, of faith, and has often been an instrument of social and political direction. The *minbar,* or pulpit, from which it is delivered, is developed from the platform, or raised dais, where the Prophet gave his decisions and directives. Some issues around the contemporary preacher will be reached in Chapter 7. It is when the sermon ends that the mosque comes fully alive in the corporateness of the prayer.

Its architecture reinforces the same lessons as the postures of the body. It is bare of distracting intrusions of artistry and exists primarily neither as an auditorium for listeners, nor as a setting for liturgy as drama. It is essentially an essay in religious space: by definition it is a place for prostration. Hence the carpets and the unencumbered expanses of area, whether domed or pillared. The niche, or *miḥrāb,* is not a sanctuary. It is merely a mark of direction, a sign of the radius of the circle of which Mecca is the center. Calligraphy, or script, and color, are the only decoration. Only that sacred text has power to solemnize the context and is immune from the menace of distraction and the distortion of unity that beset representational art. The mosque, it might be said, is the architectural service and counterpart of a devotion consistent with Islam.

But it is not finally to these things that the ultimate achievement of the liturgy is owed. It lies in the corporate piety of the generations and the sharp sacrament of the body in which it takes shape. The individual is one with the centuries in that he renews with his own immediacy of day and hour the routine of all the Prophet's people from that one beginning. This is the historical unity of a single form of words in a single liturgical language. He does so in geographical unity with the whole territory of Islam, by the conscious symbol of the *Qiblah,* the Meccan focus of the prayer, which gathers him in a great circuit, concentrically dispersed, signified as one by the sign of the *miḥrāb* inward and the token of the salutation around to right and left. It is also a local unity, whether in the ranks of the Friday concourse, or in the identity of the pattern among scattered groups of single persons in the presence-to-each-other which the sense of the mosque provides. It is, finally, a private unity of the individual, in the actions of the physical, and the intentions of the mental, part of him. These together are the answer if we ask to know the strength of Muslim piety. To bring the brow to the ground is the better to walk the earth. In prostration the Muslim learns to be erect.

The essence of *Ṣalāt,* then, is the sense of God, the reiterated practice of a religious awareness. This "remembrance" of God is known in Islam as *Dhikr*—a term which in mysticism becomes technical but which properly is inclusive of Islam as a whole. It is closely linked with ritual prayer. Thus Surah 7:206: "Remember your Lord in your soul with humility and reverence and without ostentation. Do so at morn and at eventide, and do not be negligent." It is in fact only by Quranic implication that prayer is fivefold daily. Morning and evening and a "midmost prayer" are mentioned. The recollection of God is the crucial thing, the saying of the invocation: "In the Name of God, the merciful Lord of mercy," known as the *Bismillāh.* Surah 33:42 enjoins: "O ye who have believed, mention your Lord much and praise him early and late." This act of *dhikr* is responsive to the will and mercy of God in the revelation. The Qur'ān is in several places described by the same term. It is God's self-mention, His "reminder" to men that they may be mindful of His ways, and claims. *Ṣalāt* practices this recollection with a will to the sort of awareness of God the Qur'ān teaches and evokes. "Remember Me," reads Surah 2:153, "and I will remember you: be thankful toward Me and do not belie Me."

There is a remarkable emphasis here and one that is easily missed by students of the Qur'ān, namely the antithesis between gratitude and "atheism," between *shukr* and *kufr.* The latter is a very familiar term having to do with the denial of God. But it is not only, or even mainly, contrasted with belief. Instead, here and elsewhere, it is opposed to thankfulness. The clue is that the essential atheism is not to deny God—that may be despair or honest doubt—but to ignore Him as if He were dead or gone. Or, conversely, the core of religion is not proposition but recognition. The meaning of faith in God is, in the end, not a thesis to defend but a gratitude to confess, a profound thankfulness for existence which knows that its proper dimensions are all-compelling. When the Qur'ān ponders human attitudes to God it remarks with an eloquent simplicity: "Most of them never give thanks." *Dhikr,* as the gist of *Ṣalāt,* disowns and reverses this "gracelessness of man."

As such, it spells a quality of security and peace. "The Name of the Lord is a strong tower" in the sense that the invocation of God banishes false reliances, annuls the purview of the gods of superstition, asserts an emotional dependence on God alone which liberates from other fears and cares. It hallows times and places and sets them under the single, and sufficient, rule of God against all other powers.

The theological problem of the Names of God we have already considered in Chapter 1. The religious feasibility there sustained is what *Ṣalāt* and the

Bismillāh presuppose. It is still more widely applied in various extended forms of nonritual prayer, or *du'ā'*. But in either context, it is important to understand why so much of Muslim devotion—to the puzzlement of some Christian observers—seems to ask for so little. This forbearing to make petition can, by other criteria than the Islamic, be mistaken for lack of confidence, formalism, or even insincerity. What avails it, we may query, to say: *Yā Allāh,* or *Yā Rabb,* "O God! O Lord!" and *Yā Laṭīf,* "O kindly One," and then fail to make petition? The Islamic answer is that invocation *is* petition—all the petition that is needful. One is simply asking God to be Himself. If one calls upon God as "provider" or "compassionate," one does not need to specify what His being such will mean or require, in detail, responsively to my so calling on Him. His wisdom being infinite, no discretion of mine can elaborate the cry itself. For this seeks quite adequately, in the Name alone, the answer of what God is. So "remember God" says the Qur'ān, steadily, habitually, modestly, insistently, and reverently. For "in the mention of God the hearts (of men) come to tranquillity" (Surah 13:28). "God suffices as guardian" is the sentiment of many passages. The word there yields the idea of *tawakkul,* or confident trust, an inner reliance of heart that has come to rest in the entire dependability of the One within all the Names.

That characteristic temper of *Ṣalāt* and other prayer, as a quality of those who "remember God," is told in another way if we note that many of the Names by which He is recollected have essentially to do with the crises, the cycles, of mortal existence. They are, in that sense, existential rather than metaphysical symbols. God brings to life and brings to death, nurtures and "mortalizes," provides and sustains, gives and takes, opens and closes, grants and withholds, begins and ends. Responsively to this, there are frequent Muslim prayers, often of the terse and ejaculatory kind, for the major events of life, for childbirth and circumcision, for marriage, sickness and death, for journeys, arrivals and farewells, and also for the more habitual and prosaic occasions—rising and sleeping, eating and cohabiting. Some have a devout formula for the functions of the body and the blessings of a good digestion. Setting out to travel one may say:

> O God, we ask of Thee during this our journey, righteousness and faithfulness to duty and the doing of deeds to Thee well pleasing. Thou art the companion of the road and the guardian of the family.

Or when riding and driving, in terms which might well fit any "technologizing" of daily life:

> "Glory be to Him Who made this subservient to us . . . surely to our Lord is our returning."[1]

The preoccupation with death and the beyond figures impressively in the devotion of Muslims. This mirrors, no doubt, the sharp and insistent concern of the Qur'ān with the theme of personal judgment and Heaven and Hell. It also reflects the indeterminate nature of destiny and of mercy. "Let me die a Muslim" captures this temper of knowing what is needful but not presuming to have it, and does so with a haunting kind of directness and simplicity.

In the same context one may well note the recurrent cry for refuge that belongs with all Muslim religion. This *Ta'wīdh,* or "refuge seeking" as it is known, is best pondered in the two closing chapters of the Qur'ān. It is refuge, always, *in* God, by virtue of one or other of His attributes, and it is refuge *from* evils of every kind, inward and outward, temporal and eternal, human and demonic.

Dhikr, like the meaning of *Ṣalāt* and all other devotion in Islam, is not complete without reference to one vital term, namely "intention." The daily prayers, together with all the pillars of religion, are properly prefaced by the phrase, on the lips of the individual: "I have intended the prayer of the dawn," or: "I have intended (this day) the fast of Ramaḍān." Without this confessed intention the form, though otherwise perfect and complete, would not be valid. Merely to rehearse the words of the *Shahadah* without intending to confess them would not amount to a ritual confession. To travel to Mecca in the right month is, of itself, no pilgrimage. This doctrine of the *Niyyah,* this self-alertedness we might almost call it, serves to obviate what is negligent or perfunctory, even if, in the frailties of human nature, one sometimes has to take care to intend the intention. Heedlessness, anywhere, has a way of overtaking even its own preventives.

The study of *Dhikr* has its richest fields among the Sufis who, through the centuries from the eighth, formed a vital part of Muslim existence. For Sufism, or mysticism, brought the practice of Divine remembrance to a highly deliberate, even technical, art, by cultic forms of spiritual concentration and by passionate loyalty to masters or saints of such practice, around whose persons or legends the Sufi fraternities gathered.

The first factor in this story was the arguable example of Muḥammad himself, whom the Qur'ān, in Surahs 73 and 74, describes as "enmantled," or "enwrapped." As early as the eighth century, there were mystics, like the famous woman saint Rābi'ah, of Basrah (d. 801 A.D.), and Dhū al Nūn, of Egypt (d. 861 A.D.), who sought in mystic contemplation the quality of spiritual absorption in the Divine which the Prophet had known in his experience of revelation. Did his engirdling cloak or mantle not serve as a means to, and a symbol of, his being "hidden" with the word or spirit from God? The "journey" by rapture, spoken of in Surah 17:1, might be understood in the same sense. Where ordinary tradition, as we saw, desired to conform to Muḥammad's patterns in general moral behavior, the Sufis aspired to "imitate" him in the very core of his spirituality.

There was, of course, no suggestion of further Qur'ān. Scriptural finality was impregnable. The hope, simply, was to conform to the direction of will and posture of soul, to which, in Muḥammad's case alone, the Scripture had been granted. The mystics were eager to follow a careful pattern of existential devotion to the Prophet's example.

A further factor in the emergence of the Sufis was revulsion at the moral laxities and luxuries of the Umayyad Caliphate in its metropolis at Damascus —compromises which anti-Umayyad historians probably exaggerated, but which were dismaying enough to provoke political unrest and theological questioning,[2] as well as the characteristically mystical reaction which determined to find a countering personal austerity. This repudiation of the pervasive worldliness of "establishment" Islam in the eighth century is the probable explanation of the term *Ṣūfī,* which is derived from *ṣūf* (wool). For wool rebuked, in its plain simplicity, the silks and satins of the Damascus court, the affluence and indulgence which had forsaken the primitive discipline of the first disciples and companions of Muḥammad. Sufism, in this sense, meant "other-worldliness" against "this-worldliness." It gave warm and intimate expression to Muslim religion both in ardent personal form and, by later development, in local brotherhoods of discipline.

It was also stimulated by a sense of latent discontent with the aridity of dogma by the tenth and eleventh centuries A.D. Some factors in the negative theology we have already noted. On several of the major themes—God and unity, man and will, the status of the Qur'ān, the nature of faith, and the role of reason—a habit of scholasticism developed with a love of abstraction and evasive subtlety. Sufism through the centuries provided a welcome haven from these embittering contentions and attracted those wistful or sceptical souls who find the ambitions of reason dubious or overweening even when they are soundly exercised.

Among the greatest of the early Sufis were Al-Muḥāsibī (d. 837 A.D.) and Al-Junaid (d. 910 A.D.). The most tragic was certainly Al-Ḥallāj, executed by crucifixion in 922 A.D., for his misconstrued ecstacy of Divine union. Baghdad was the center of all these, but its greatest figure and the supreme architect of Sufi thought was the celebrated Al-Ghazālī (d. 1111 A.D.). His monumental work, with the title (literally rendered): "The Revival of the Sciences of Religion," was quoted in Chapter 1. It was in fact a thoroughgoing study of what might be called "The Art of Being Islamic," and an extraordinary compendium of profound spiritual and psychological insight. He himself had come to a quality of theology involving a deep personal revolt against scholastic rationalism, and yet clothing the Sufi ardor in patient, disciplined thought. The story of Al-Ghazālī's renunciation of Baghdad and intellectual careerism and his long pilgrimage of spiritual search remains a supreme classic of Islamic religion. His eminence gave powerful reinforcement, as well as good repute, to the Sufi movement. It was in default of such leadership that its history tells a more chequered story as it comes closer to the modern period.

Yet no one had more clearly diagnosed the temptations of the would-be Sufi or charted his path of disciplined vocation than Al-Ghazālī. That path, already known as the *Tarīqah,* lay in a life of devotion, usually shared by a cult group or brotherhood committed to its practice though there were also solitaries. The word means "a way," "a path of going," and signifies a soul-progress from the temporal to the eternal, from the self preoccupied to the true being, from sin to God. The goal was differently interpreted, whether as periodic realization of the Divine glory from which the soul should return to mundane existence in the illumination of the experience, or as a passing away of self-centric being in the unbroken unity of God. It was the latter that Al-Ḥallāj had sought and claimed in the famous, and tragic, sentence for which he was crucified: *Anā-l-Ḥaqq,* "I am the Truth," "I am the Real." He was taken to be blaspheming in presuming to an "individual" identity with God—the most flagrant degree of *Shirk*. What in fact he meant, beyond the perception or the malice of his foes to apprehend, was that in his awareness of truth he had passed the frontier of a subject/object religion into a mystical *Tauḥīd,* the unity which is not the exterior assertion of a unitary "He" but the beatific confession of the unitive "We."

That goal, however understood, necessitated a prolonged discipleship in the "Way," leading through stages and their corresponding states, towards the destination. There was the seeker, the wayfarer, and the initiate—the three categories, broadly understood, of Sufi experience. Their movement of soul was from acquisitiveness to renunciation, from pride to humility, from anxiety to inner peace, from love of abundance to contentment with adversity. This inner progress was often linked with the idea of *Jihād,* inwardly interpreted as being a struggle "in the way of God," having its beginning in the turning of the heart or *taubah,* meaning a conversion of concern. This inaugurated the sustained search after self-abnegation, patience, fear, solitude, abstinence, and the sense of the Divine *murāqabah* ("Thou, God, seest me"). Prospered by the Spirit and by steadfastness these were rewarded by the knowledge and love of God.

The stages and states differed between varying masters of the way, and precise analysis defeats itself. What mattered was the hunger of the heart and the reality of self-surrender. Al-Ghazālī's autobiography, known as "The Deliverer from Wandering" yields us the most worthy and illuminating narrative.

> I . . . turned with set purpose to the method of mysticism (or Sufism). I knew that the complete mystic 'way' includes both intellectual belief and practical activity; the latter consists in getting rid of the obstacles in the self and its stripping off its base characteristics and vicious morals, so that the heart may attain to freedom from what is not God and to constant recollection of Him.

After full study, he continued:

> It was clear to me that the key to all this was to sever the attachment of the heart to worldly things by leaving the mansion of deception and returning to that of eternity, and to advance towards God most high with all earnestness . . .

> I realised that I was caught in a veritable thicket of attachments . . . I examined my motive in my work of teaching and realized that it was not a pure desire for the things of God, but that the moving impulse moving me was the desire for an influential position and public recognition. I saw for certain that I was on the brink of a crumbling bank of sand and in imminent danger of hell-fire unless I took my state in hand . . . I sought refuge with God most high as one who is driven to him because he has no other resource . . . He made it easy for me to turn away from position and wealth, from children and friends.[3]

This was Sufi interiority at its noblest. Its exterior organization takes us to the numerous Sufi Orders which flourished from the twelfth century until modern times. They were formed in each case around a master from whom, for the most part, they took their name and who established a common discipline and made current a particular ritual or form of *Dhikr*. Other factors entered into their genesis and their vitality, both economic and social. They gave communal solidarity to their members and spiritual shape to trade interests and craft guilds and other local brotherhoods. The earliest great Order was the Jilāniyyah, founded by Al-Jilānī (d. 1078). Subsequently came the Suhrawardiyyah, the Shādhiliyyah, and the Maulawiyyah, with its famous Maulana (or Mevlevi) Jalāl al-Dīn Rūmī (d. 1273).

The cultic patterns varied. *Taṣawwuf,* or the art of being a Sufi, lent itself to a wide diversity of technique and emotion. One of the extremest forms was the whirling practiced by the Mevlevis, whose dervishes induced an ecstatic concentration on God by the rapid, rhythmic movement of the body. The use of long recitation of the word *Allāh,* or elaborations of the *Takbīr* (i.e., saying: "God is most great") or the use of the *Taṣliyah* and the *Ta'wīdh* in swaying chant and sequence, as well as endless other means, gave to the Orders in their local "cells" or groups both an intense experience of community and an access, in some sort, to the world of *al-Ghaib,* as their masters knew and told it —the world of unseen reality, the true home of the disciple.

Sufism served to enrich Islam with many strains of cultural and social expression and liberated its common folk into a self-transcending intensity of spiritual life they could have reached in no other way. With its manifold energies of soul, its strenuous demands and its vast diffusion through the lands and centuries of Islam, the life of the Sufi Orders might be broadly described as the Islamic counterpart of Christian monasticism, without of course its altars, and, in the main, without its walls, its celibacy and its cloisters.

They had something too, in characteristically different Islamic terms, of the monastic distinctiveness. The pursuit of sanctity has always been, by implication, a reproach of society. Sufi patterns of initiation and discipleship qualified the egalitarianism of Muslim *Ṣalāt.* They often related uneasily also to the custodians of dogma. For by their very nature they held loosely to the letter and even to the routine claims of *Dīn,* if these seemed to impede the "private" discipline. They were at times prone to spiritualize the pilgrimage and the fast. When degeneracy overtook them they became a prey to charlatans.

But on all counts their long and vital role in Islam is eloquent both of the needs it measured and the resources it possessed. Despite all its contemporary stresses, Sufism remains a hopeful factor in the interreligious relations of Islam. Mystics are always easier neighbors than dogmatists.

We are not turning from our central clue of *Dhikr,* now explored in its Sufi reaches, when we move in the study of Islamic liturgy to Fasting and Pilgrimage. With the theme of *Ṣalāt,* and its bearings, now complete, and with *Zakāt* and the *Shahādah* studied elsewhere, the Ramaḍān fast and the *Ḥajj* to Mecca conclude the elements of *Dīn.*

These, equally with *Ṣalāt,* are institutions of man's responsive awareness of God. As enjoined, their performance fulfills the obligation God has set for men. That alone makes them an obedient cognizance of Him. Fasting incorporates—in an almost literal sense of the word—the same principle as the bodily movements in *Ṣalāt,* namely the physical sacrament.

Ramaḍān means complete abstinence from dawn to sunset. To transfer food taking and drinking from the day to the night hours, it may be argued, has no logic to uphold it, but is quite arbitrary and highly inconvenient, though less so perhaps, in the Hijāz of the seventh century, than now. But this is to be merely rational. The *imsāk,* as the term goes, the "withholding" of the body from its natural satisfactions from dawn till dusk reminds it, compellingly, of a Divine claim and imposes a pattern of discipline that educates and habituates it for other tasks and realms. The communal atmosphere that Ramaḍān provides powerfully reinforces the collective sense of Muslims, sets them a sort of sacramental sign of oneness, and affords, as experience confirms, an effectual way of becoming Muslim simply by making occasion for participant adherence. There are many whose Islam begins in the month of Ramaḍān, finds its genesis in a day abstinence and a night meal, and is thereby recruited into Muslim standing, however untaught it may remain. This is the real logic of the fast.

That distinguishing mark was certainly the initial character of the fast at its institution. The Quranic directive came in the following terms shortly after the emigration from Mecca:

> O believers, prescribed for you is the Fast, for days numbered . . . the month of Ramaḍān wherein the Qur'ān was sent down for a guidance to the people. . . . Eat and drink until the white streaks show clearly to you from the black streaks in the dawn, then continue the Fast until the night . . . while you keep to the mosques (Surah 2:183–187).

It is often seen by historians as the most notable of several developments within the Islamic community, marking a conscious independence of other religions' norms. Ramaḍān differed from both Jewish and Christian fasting, in its twenty-eight day period and its daylight incidence, and in its disconnection from other elements such as redemption or atonement. The Muslim fast is understood, classically, as an absolute prohibition of all bodily sustenance by whatever means and an abstinence from sexual activity. It is a time of intensified devotion and mutual forgiveness. The hardships it imposes, particularly when the cycle of the lunar calendar brings it round into the heat of summer, are to be taken in the stride of loyalty.

That sheer physical strenuousness, however, is less problematic than the issues raised by the letter of the fast in the context of modern industrial and mechanized society. Just as the din of traffic and the rush of cities tend to drown the call to prayer and the preoccupations of work, of shift systems, and the rest, disrupt the fivefold prayers, so the demands of transport, trade, and technology impede the fasting capabilities of many sections of the modern community. Whereas loud-speakers and electronic devices on the minarets can help surmount the competition of the streets, there is no external solution to the dilemma of Ramaḍān-keeping where efficiency competes with it. There have been moves, notably in Tunisia under President Bourguiba, to reinterpret the fast as an inner discipline to be observed, not by a literal loyalty, but by a creative acceptance of its meaning. Ramaḍān is then a confession of the duty of the flesh to serve, and never to engross, the spirit. Islam, says this view, cannot be held to a literalism, feasible only for an economy that has gone into the limbo of the past and thus inappropriate to a dynamic and enduring faith. Even in Surah 2, exigencies of sickness or travel allow a making good of the fast at another time. May not sterner exigencies admit its fulfillment in another idiom?

Others, by contrast, though taking the point of the dilemma, protest that the fast is in fact more viable, even today, than these radical ideas argue. But, more important, they see every spiritual interpretation as needing the anchor of the ordinance, the sacrament of the literal demand. A fast of the mind is no substitute for the reality of the foodless days, the regimen of their full sequence, the hard, experienced fact in its full rigor. Without these, men never know the release, the spontaneous joy, of the nightly comradeship, the sense of achievement and belonging, and the benign satisfaction of the *'Īd al-Fitr,* or "feast of the breaking," with which the fast ends.

Statistics are elusive and impressions precarious. But there is no reason to doubt that in the wide stretches of *Dār al-Islām,* and through all its diverse peoples, the observance of Ramaḍān is deeply felt. Since childhood is exempt, the first keeping of it often marks a memorable sort of initiation into Islam for boys and girls on the threshold of their teens, or earlier. It has an impact all can understand and, though listlessness may be part of the price as the long day wears on, the solidarity and the exactingness that arise from Ramaḍān at least ensure that religion is not negligible. In sensitive quarters, whether radical or conservative, the Islamic mind is aware of the snares of formalism, and meritoriousness, which accompany all religious obligations, and the most rigorous of them most of all.

The final pillar of religion, the *Ḥajj,* gives a yearly fulfillment, in travel, to the symbol of the *Qiblah* in *Ṣalāt.* From the local mosque the lines radiate inwards to their focal point in Mecca: in the pilgrimage the faithful make their way down them to the central shrine. The *miḥrāb* is no pointer on an untravelled road. By this annual "congregation" Islam is bound together in a visible sacrament of unity, geographically realized from the ends of the earth. In history the pilgrimage has profoundly served the solidarity of Islam and helped to a strong cosmopolitanism in architecture, tradition, and society, through the contacts it afforded. Each recurring year it mediates through the body of the faithful a vicarious experience of the symbol of Mecca, in that pilgrims share with their neighbors the thrill and emotion of their venture both in retrospect and prospect. In the actuality of the ceremonies themselves in and about Mecca there resides a powerful realization of the incorporate community of Islam, in time and place.

The Quranic directive is in Surah 2:196–97, which says, simply, "Fulfill the pilgrimage and the visitation unto God." The phrase: "But if you are prevented . . ." has occasioned long, exegetical discussion as to legitimate inability. But there is no doubt that a resolute will to pilgrimage is the Muslim's bounden duty. "He who can find a way thither"—to quote 3:97—must do so. To find a corporate and perpetual way there had been the crucial theme of all Muḥammad's policy after the *Hijrah*. That he did so was his most signal victory and the *Ḥajj* is simply its perpetuation into the texture of Islamic emotion in annual renewal. The continuity within Islam of Mecca's role as a city sanctuary terminated all ambiguity about the effect of his mission against idols on the status of their central shrines. It also cleansed and rehabilitated the familiarly sacred territory itself, islamized, as it were, the very symbol of the struggle, making the triumph complete. The individual pilgrim, surmounting his own circumstantial obstacles, is treading the same road.

He is also presenting himself before God in the spirit of Abraham, who, with Ishmael, is believed to have been the founder and builder of Mecca. By this criterion as Muḥammad saw it, the polytheists of the city were usurpers. The cleansing of the *Ka'bah*—the central sanctuary in the great house of pilgrimage at Mecca—had been its repossession, by Muḥammad's arms, in the name of truth.

The Muslim's pilgrimage opens with the *Niyyah,* or "intention," as he draws near to the city, which he greets with the cry: *Labbaiḳa:* "Here am I, Lord, here am I." By these words, the servant presents himself before God at the rendezvous of revelation and of community. There follows the *Tawāf,* or rite of circumambulation around the *Ka'bah,* which stands, cube-shaped, in the center of the mosque court. During the circuits he stretches arms and breast against the "black stone" and kisses it. The stone, set in the *Ka'bah* wall, is an object of very ancient veneration. The *Ṭawāf* is only undertaken in the state of *Iḥrām,* or "solemn hallowing," as the ritual condition of the entire pilgrimage. Its symbol is the pilgrim garb and it sets apart for the special purpose of the rites both the period and the person, requiring abstinence from sexuality and from trade. The circuits of the *Ka'bah* are followed by *sa'y,* or running seven times, to and fro, through one of the principal thoroughfares of Mecca towards Marwa, a distance in all of almost two miles, recalling the desperate search of Hagar for water for her son, Ishmael.

The climax comes between the eighth and the tenth day of pilgrimage, with the journey, through Mina, five miles eastward of Mecca, to the plain of ʿArafāt, nine miles beyond it. After a night en route the whole pilgrim concourse "stands" from noon to near sunset at ʿArafāt, recalling, with the aid of sermons, or *k̲hutbahs,* the *wuqūf,* or "standing" of Abraham, the great iconoclast, staunch against idolatry. Then, at sunset, the passage to Muzdalīfah, halfway towards Mecca, for the night, and on the next day the "stoning" at Mina, which recalls Abraham's rejection of the evil Satan. The pilgrims cast seven stones at a low pillar in the main square of Mina, in repudiation of the archrejector of the Divine will.[4]

The pilgrimage proper ends with the sacrifice at Mina of animals in ritual slaughter. These ceremonies, known as the *ʿĪd al-Aḍḥā,* or *Al-ʿĪd al-Kabir,* or *Bairām,* have their counterpart in every devout Muslim household. The simultaneous, universal character of the rite with which pilgrimage is complete makes for a powerful, vicarious sense of its significance. The consecrated animal, provided either by each pilgrim for himself, or in groups, is slaughtered with its head towards Mecca. Part of the flesh is eaten by the worshippers, part distributed and part left at the place of slaughter. This climax of the *manāsik̲,* or pilgrim obligations, is followed by a shaving of the head and a partial desacrilization. The state of *Iḥrām* finally ends after the last circuit of the *Kaʿbah.*

There is a lesser pilgrimage or *ʿUmrah,* distinct from the *Ḥajj* proper, which may be performed at any time and which does not include the journey to ʿArafāt. Throughout the ceremonies there are ejaculatory prayers as in *Ṣalāt,* and four official *k̲huṭbahs,* or sermons, are delivered. Pilgrims may also include Medina in their travels and do honor to the Prophet's grave. But these devotions are outside the pilgrimage itself as also are the various salutations at the tombs in the Meccan vicinity. Home-bound pilgrims traditionally take with them water from the well of Zamzam, the holy spring in Mecca where Hagar saved her life and Ishmael's in their distress.

They also take the memory of a deep religious transaction, an encounter with history and with the world-community of which they are part. Modern conditions have gone far to alleviate the old risks and rigors of the *Ḥajj.* The trials and fears of earlier generations of Mecca-seekers have passed into history. But there remains, unique to Islam and only for the Muslim, the pull of its single magnetism, reaching to the corners of the earth. It is the terrestrial sign of the *Ummah.* To that we must now turn.

Quranic Passages to Study

Surahs 1; 2:45–46, 142–145, 183–197; 16:1–24; 17:78–79; 20:130–136; 22:27–39; 30:17–60; 33:35–36; and Surah 67.

Some Questions

1. "So remember thy Lord." How is this central imperative of Islam achieved?
2. What are the elements which give Muslim prayer its unique character and quality?
3. "If hunger is its only result, the Fast is not a true one." Why?
4. Assess the Pilgrimage as a sacrament both of devotion and of unity.
5. What are the sources and the achievements of Sufism?

6.
Ummah

Cohesion and a sense of solidarity are vital factors in the continuity of great religions. In Islam they belong with the fact and concept of the *Ummah*—a term which is difficult to translate into one single, English equivalent. It has elements of "nation," "community," "people," and "religion"—all fused into characteristic Islamic quality and ideal. *Ummah,* we might say, is the collective dimension belonging to Muslims, in the trust of the Qur'ān, the obedience of Muḥammad and the fulfillment of law and liturgy.

"We did not find our ancestors in such ways," said the Prophet's townsmen in Mecca, in rejection of his preaching. (Surahs 2:170; 5:104 and 10:78.) "Our fathers," they went on, were (literally) "upon a community," that is, "of an *Ummah.*" That corporate loyalty the pagans did not intend to abandon at the call of an upstart.

Already, then, in the earliest encounter, was this tradition of the collective, the living and the dead, in religion. Beyond all their commercial instincts lay their anxiety for the persistence of the tribal worship. By the same token, Muḥammad's goal had to be a new *Ummah,* unitary in worship, supratribal and decisive. The clear active enunciation of this policy, its crucial point of departure, was the *Hijrah,* by which Muḥammad and his community left Mecca and established in Medina. It is from that watershed of development, appropriately, that the Islamic calendar begins.[1] Historians saw in it the real hinge of Muslim genesis. It is striking that they did not locate the date of definition either in the birth of Muḥammad or in the initiation of the Qur'ān. Where Muslims, who were already his disciples, were faced with a decision to emigrate and throw in their lot with a cause against their own kin from a center outside—there the Islamic era opens. This was, in its critical quality, a bigger decision than a confession of faith or the endurance of the community's hostility while still resident within it. Faith-solidarity was now actively pitted against blood-kinship.

This was the decisive thing. Some modern writers see in it the emergence of a new personalism destined to transform the Arab mentality. If this be too romantic a view, it was certainly a basic revision of tribalism, a new pattern of priority. This was the new *Ummah* implicit in the *Hijrah.* The emigrants were cast upon the aid and comfort of "alien" Medinan partners and involved in separation, material and emotional, from their kindred left in Mecca. That there were some kinship ties within Medina does not diminish what was meant by an espousal of new citizenship.

But the new *Ummah,* founded in unitary religion, was not just another "tribe." By those religious origins it was committed to all compatible access of membership. Its first postures were necessarily alert and militant. For the situation was liable to subterfuge. Jeopardy was its "native air." Medina, moreover, was at first only partially secure and had to be consolidated into identity of interest with Muḥammad and the non-Muslim Medinans persuaded, cajoled or maneuvred, into the cause which, if it did not now "make" their city, would certainly, by failure, unmake it, through Meccan retaliation. The narrative of that consolidation we need not retell: its political and military opportunism we have already noted. The build-up of resources, the worsting of Quraishī power and counsels, the campaign of arms and negotiation leading to its capitulation, are a classic story of successful leadership.

Throughout, even at its most militant, the open *Ummah* idea is never lost to sight. Even the *Hijrah* was not allowed to close the doors behind it. Stragglers who were ready to come late were not precluded on the ground that they had lost their chance or lacked a timely heroism. For timidity could have a change of mind, or intimidation be defied with a better courage. All sincere accession is timely.

In the sixth year of the *Hijrah,* in the armistice of Al-Ḥudaibiyyah, Muḥammad negotiated the first pilgrimage to Mecca of Islam as such, the Quraish agreeing to evacuate the city for three days, the next year, for this purpose. More adherence accrued from its consequences than from thirteen years of preaching. The prestige of negotiating with the Quraish as an equal, the symbolic value of the pilgrimage to be made, the ten-year freedom of either party to make what alliances they wished (thus affording cover for acceding tribes)—all these far outweighed the concession by which he dropped the title of *Rasūl-Allāh* from his formal style in the document—a concession which angered and dismayed his less perceptive followers. For the substance of the *Rasūliyyah* was emphatically set forward.

When, by these military and diplomatic measures, Mecca was finally conquered and incorporated into Islam, there were two historic capitals, the city of the preaching and the city of the power. The *Ummah* of Islam acquired thereby an abiding sign of its supralocal, intertribal character. There were soon to be a score of cities. Mecca was quickly and almost painlessly brought into the fold. The idols did not die hard. They surrendered, the historian may say, in the human surrender of their city. Therein is both fact and symbol. It was power which brought the Quraish to heel: but it was power generated by and for a faith about God needing no city for refuge and claiming all cities for empire. Islam had become a state. Their mutual victory was indivisible.

It was soon to seem everywhere repeatable. Some time after Mecca's capitulation and during the steady, if not always unchallenged, Islamization within Arabia, Muḥammad sent letters to rulers in the world of that day, to Byzantium,

Egypt, and Ethiopia, requiring their adhesion to Islam. It is suggested in some quarters that if they had agreed to let their peoples embrace the Muslim faith and liturgy, their political authorities would have been preserved intact in their hands. We can only imagine how Islam would then have been organized, with politically "independent" national accessions and no *Jihād,* or religious war, ever proclaimed and pursued. Islam, existing thus religiously under a variety of persisting sovereignties, would not have been the great *Dār al-Islām* that history knows. Mecca had set the precedent for religio-political surrender and the external world was to learn the same pattern.

The main interest of the tradition about the letters is the implicit: *Cuius regio, eius religio* principle—the summons of rulers to the faith as the key to their peoples' adherence. In rejecting or ignoring Muḥammad's letter, its recipients had no notion of the incredible sequence that history held in store. They could not have known that the new Islamic *Ummah* was poised for massive victories altogether phenomenal in their reach and finality.

Our concern here with the story of the expansion that brought Islam across North Africa, the Straits of Gibraltar, and the Pyrenees, and far into eastern Asia, within a century of the Prophet's death, is more for its deep consequences in the religious temper of Islam than for its dramatic chronology in detail. At the accession of the second Caliph, 'Umar, in 634 A.D. the whole Arabian peninsula had been won. At his death in 644 A.D., Egypt and Libya to the west had been conquered, and, northward and eastward, the Fertile Crescent, Syria, Iraq, and Persia as far as Hamadan and Isfahan. The third Caliph, 'Uthmān (644–656 A.D.), continued the advance westward into Tripolitania, northward through Armenia and on to the Caucasus Mountains and eastward into Khuzistan and the borders of Afghanistan. Under the early Umayyads, the Maghrib (Tunis, Algeria, and Morocco) and Spain, almost to the Pyrenees, were added to the Muslim realm. The tide in Europe was only turned, in the heart of France by Charlemagne in 732, at the Battle of Tours, exactly one century after Muḥammad's death. It continued to flow in the east as far as Sind and the Indus River. The tale, and the enemy toll, of battles, the collapse of great Byzantine and Persian provinces, the military prowess of 'Umar himself, of Khālid and Amrū and other famous generals, the very yielding, as it seemed, of history, to the Muslim will—all these gave to Islam the habit of assurance and the instinct of dominion. History itself had become tributary to Muslim destiny and all its other peoples and beliefs their subjects.

The religious "logic" of the Islamic expansion takes in its stride the underlying factors of historical explanation. The first was the *élan vital*—as the French might say—of the Muslim armies, their unfailing ardor, their inner zest. Muḥammad had touched the deepest springs of valor and sanctified them in the notion of *Jihād,* making the living as invulnerable and the fallen as already immortal in the heavens. "In the way of God" was the phrase from which their temper drew its strength and generated what nothing mercenary could match. Rather it dispirited all that blocked its way—forces which were already undermined by the long contentions of the Byzantine and Persian Empires, by the restiveness of the border provinces, by the heavy grievances of the populations and the enfeebling controversies within eastern Christendom. In places the Muslims' successes owed as much to the welcome of the conquered as to the weight of the conquerors.

There were also in the reckoning powerful economic factors—the attraction of the cultured lands that proved so readily reducible, the pressures of poverty and numbers within the Arabian peninsula. There had been earlier eruptions of the "desert" into "the sown." But the seventh century had the indefinable, unprecedented factor of Islam to fuse all else into irresistibility. The experience, in turn, gave Islam a corroboration of finality and a freehold on power.

It also opened to it a vast influx of new adherence, new peoples and old cultures, with their customs and traditions, to be absorbed into the Islamic whole. But the assurance of that advent and its sanctions of supremacy were such as to bring them effectively into Muslim mold. Islam in turn gained a new sophistication both of mind and doctrine, by contact with dimensions of being unknown in its hearthland. It became heir to Plato and Aristotle and to the metaphysical aspirations of the Greek temper. Its theology responded to influences deriving from the long preoccupations of the Christian faith and developed its own form of the problem of Divine and human will, of faith and works, and of the status of the word of God in the Quranic Scripture.

But its reactions of receptivity in all these myriad ways never yielded the essential definition which the origins of Islam had given. Hospitality there was, together with ambivalence, yet always within a capacity to preserve and impose the inner identity. It was not the sword, in the sharp and naked sense, in ruthlessness and anger, that made its triumph. Any such thesis grossly oversimplifies and distorts the story. The authority of empire is the proper summary of the means of its displacement both of potentates and faiths. Islam did not speak from catacombs, for it told only what it knew in its own emergence, and it assumed that its reception should conform to that same experience. It saw the way of truth as passing always through thrones. There was, therefore, a reciprocal relation between conversion and submission, between conquest and *Ṣalāt*. How, indeed, should it be otherwise? But it reserved its intolerance only for idolatry and all defiance of the God Who had empowered it.

Immensely multiplied and diversified from Spain to the Indus River and beyond, the history of the *Ummah* is outside our scope here. The interpenetration of Islam with cultures, Asian, Indian, Malayan, Indonesian, African, needs encyclopedic telling. We concentrate on the idea itself, its caliphal order, its Sunnī-Shī'ah cleavage and the way it had with tolerated minorities.

As briefly noted in Chapter 2, the institution of the Caliphate had already been created in the immediate aftermath of Muḥammad's death. Under the second Caliph, 'Umar, it became the most formidable of thrones. For long in practice, and always in theory, it constituted a symbolic headship of the community, believed through the tradition to have Divine sanction. It provided a focus of allegiance and embodied, among other implications, two general truths of the Islamic *Ummah,* namely the subject's duty of total obedience and the ruler's obligation of "representativeness" under God. "Representativeness" is deliberately used, at some risk, in this context. It is not that the Caliphate was ever popularly elective in a suffrage sense, but that its holder was to be the first of those who pray and the executant, not the author, of the sacred *Sharī'ah.*

The second of these aspects is more easily told. Muḥammad had personally led the prayers in the post-*Hijrah* community. He prostrated at the *miḥrāb* as well as governed from the *minbar.* From the outset his successors followed the same habit. Wherever the Caliph was present he was the congregational leader among the faithful. The pattern became general through the lower echelons of government, provincial and local. Truly any individual, however lowly, could lead the *Ṣalāt.* The custom by which the political authority in its highest, or highest available, personage presided at the liturgy may be seen as the Islamic form of the theory of the state, of the interplay of the Divine and the temporal sovereignty. Not here the sacral kingship or the coronation of emperors, but the ritual centrality—without essential distinction of liturgical action—of the politically supreme figure. This is the Imamate inherent in the Caliphate.

It stands, also, as a token of the theoretical subservience of the Caliph to the *Sharī'ah.* He bows with the rest. He is not the Prophet, nor the Prophet's "son." Prophecy was sealed in 632, with the death of Muḥammad. The Caliph administers the law rooted in that finalized revelation, as completed by the other Divinely willed sources. The law is preserved and fulfilled under the wing of the Caliphate but it is not subdued to it. In Sunnī theory, it is the community, not the commander, of the faithful, who is the guardian and guarantor of the *Sharī'ah.* His power, however, is the condition of its operation. The Sunnī *'Ulamā',* or learned experts, were able, for the most part, to make good their claim to custody and interpretation of the law as their proper role.

The duty of the subject to the Caliph was one of implicit obedience. The Shī'ah, because of their disaffection over 'Alī and his cause, and certain other minority sects, sought, from time to time in the first two centuries of Islam, to assert a right of nonobedience. But among Sunnis, the authority of the Caliph was a paramount religious principle. From the beginning, in 632 at Muḥammad's death, there were urgent practical necessities for swift and undisputed succession. The rapid expansion of Islam in the following decades intensified this need. The weakness of 'Uthmān, the third Caliph (644–656 A.D.) and the ensuing strife under 'Alī (656–661 A.D.) underlined the same lesson. Mu'āwiya, who displaced 'Alī in 661, to found the Umayyad Caliphate, with Damascus as its center, ruled vigorously and began the practice of designating the son who was to succeed and of ensuring public recognition of him in advance. This application of the hereditary principle, which had not obtained from 632 to 661, was intended to ensure continuity of effective control and to avoid the crises of succession. It also provided for the legal requirement that the Caliph should be descended from the Quraish of Mecca.

The autocratic character of the Caliphate became more marked under the

'Abbasids, who took power from the Umayyads in 750 A.D. and ruled from Baghdad. Persian traditions of despotism supplanted the Arab ways of the Umayyads. New and more pretentious titles were assumed: "the Caliph of God" (rather than ". . . of the Apostle") and "the Shadow of God upon earth." Though they had profited from temporary alliance with disaffected elements to unseat the Umayyads, the 'Abbasids were not minded to permit a repetition of the tactic. The tendency to link centralized power with a growing emphasis on "official" orthodoxy increased in the ninth century. It coincided with the growing authority of non-Arab elements in Islamic life—a development which, while attesting its universalism, strained its unity.

The heydey of 'Abbasid power passed by the tenth century, though it continued in formal line and yielded a theoretical succession to the Ottoman Caliphate in the fifteenth century. The intervening centuries saw the rise and flux of numerous smaller and rival "caliphates" or vassalages. The territories west of Tunis, and the Spanish peninsula never in fact came into the orbit of 'Abbasid Baghdad. The Umayyads who continued there, and their successor potentates, made good a pattern of separatism that came to be general throughout the east. The vicissitudes of the Ikhshidids, the Tulūnids, the (Shī'ah) Fāṭimids, of Egypt and Tunis; the Buwayhids of Baghdad; the Ghaznawids across Persia from the Caucasus to India; the Almoravids in Spain and the Maghrib; and others of lesser range in time and place, belong to political history rather than the study of religion. But, in their turbulent sequence, and in the tensions of the Crusades in the eleventh and twelfth centuries, the tribulations of Mongol invasion in the thirteenth, the struggles of Seljuq and Ottoman Turks in the fourteenth, lies ample proof of the durability of the Islamic way and of the capacity of its inner forces to take its outward conquerors in hand. In that sense, the persistence of the *Ummah* defies admitted fragmentation and the stresses of military and cultural invasion. The other salient fact in the long story of Islam up to the sixteenth century is the contribution of the Persian and the Turkish languages to the service and adornment of its thought and meaning.

Though never after 750 A.D. a sovereignty physically coextensive with Islamic territories, the Caliphate did not cease to symbolize what it failed to embrace. It stood for the fundamental axiom of Islamic existence, namely that the state is the sign and surety of the faith and the faith is the ground and seal of the state. So it had been in the dispensation of Muḥammad, and the Caliphate was the historical perpetuation of that partnership. That it was unable to preserve effective unity through tumultuous centuries across three continents does not diminish the concept of which it was the organ.

That conclusion to this long and rapid retrospect over centuries from the Umayyads to the rise of the Ottomans will be reinforced, from another angle, when we turn to the shape of the *Ummah* in the circumstances created by the nineteenth century and by the Ottoman demise in the first quarter of the twentieth century. That perspective, like the other, does no justice to the manifold of history, but it must suffice for the thread of our concern.

Before turning to that modern dilemma, our duty is still with the immediate sequel to Muḥammad's death, in order to take due measure of Islam's primary and permanent schism. The Caliphate from 632 to 644 was a story of unity and success, in which the first two holders of the office were not challenged—though later Shī'ah theory insists that even in the first instance, in 632, 'Alī, cousin and son-in-law of Muḥammad, was wrongfully passed over. It was, however, under the third Caliph that disaffection, gathering round his claims, became bitter and open. The unrest of 'Uthmān's years (644–656 A.D.) deepened when 'Alī, in compromised circumstances, finally became Caliph in 656 A.D. Opposition to him never accepted his rule. Disaster overtook his reign and, after his murder in 661 A.D. his following, the 'Alids, could make little headway against the shrewd and determined *de facto* authority of the first Umayyad Caliph at Damascus. But on his death, the smoldering 'Alid cause erupted into brief flame, in the ill-starred venture of Ḥusain, younger son of 'Alī, who challenged the next Umayyad Caliph, Yāzīd, and was annihilated with almost his whole retinue in the massacre of Karbalā' in 680 A.D.

It was the horror of this event, coupled with the murder in 669 A.D. of the elder son of Alī, that gave the aura of martyrdom to their ill-fated house. So tragic a destiny befalling the nearest kinsmen and the only grandsons of the Prophet, cried out for the spiritual recompense of an immortal devotion, and Shī'ah Islam was born in the response. The continuing political frustrations of the 'Alid party only sharpened its intensity. Even when the Umayyad Caliphate gave way to the 'Abbāsids, their external fortunes, despite their service to the change, remained fitful and forlorn. In his lifetime 'Alī had enjoyed an ardent reputation for his chivalry and saintliness. That memory, hallowed by the pathos of his family and of Fāṭimah, his widow, took shape in a passionate, ardent allegiance. It was one of those occasions in history where mingling anger and pity, wrought into the cult of suffering, evoked a staunch refusal to forget or, by forgetfulness, to conspire with the injustices of fate and leave the spilled blood silent in the sand. It is this quality which, despite the vagaries and the divisiveness, gives Shī'ah Islam its fascination for the student of religion.

External, political privations, however, were only one factor. Underlying the Shī'ah form of Islam is a divergent concept of the guarantees of living continuity in faith. Whereas Sunnis rely broadly on the *Sharī'ah* in the community to ensure a true standing in Islam through the generations in their sequence, Shī'ahs believe in renewed mediation of Muḥammad's finality through a sequence of Imāms. These are much more than the prayer-leading figures known to Sunnī Islam. They stood in lineal relation to Muḥammad and only through them did the faithful in each generation stand within the authentic truth. The Sunnī scheme took the lengthening ages of Islam back, as it were, horizontally in the plane of history to the fountainhead in the Prophet, and bound them into one by the criterion of the *Sharī'ah*. Shī'ah Islam saw that final source linked afresh to each generation, vertically, through the Imām, without whom the faith and the faithful could not coinhere. In doing so, they did not impugn the finality of the Qur'ān: they believed they possessed it through renewed emanation of the original "light of Muḥammad." This light was guaranteed by hereditary succession and designation of the previous Imām.

The first Imām after Karbalā' was "the young 'Alī," a survivor of the massacre and son to Ḥusain, who came to be known for his piety as Zain al-'Ābidīn, "the paragon of worshippers." From him derived a succession which, numbering from 'Alī, counted seven Imāms and, for another segment of devotion, twelve Imāms. The schism between the Seveners, (*Al-Sabā 'iyyah*) and the Twelvers, (*Al-Ithnā 'Ashuriyyah*) was a central cleavage within the Shī'ah loyalty. The division came after the Imamate of Ja'far (d. 765 A.D.). The Seveners recognized Ismā'īl, Ja'far's son, who had predeceased his father and whose sect is thus known also as the Ismailis. The Twelvers took Mūsā Kāẓim, a surviving son of Ja'far, from whom the line continued until the twelfth Imām, Ḥasan al-'Askarī (d. 874 A.D.). At that point the Twelvers adopted a position comparable to that taken by the Seveners at the earlier date, namely belief in the concealment of the true Imām, to await manifestation in God's time and to guide the faithful meanwhile out of hiddenness. The hidden Imām for the Seveners was the lost son, Ismā'īl. For the Twelvers it was the son of Ḥasan al-'Askarī, who mysteriously disappeared at Samarra, about the age of seven. He may have been abducted or killed, but piety believed that he had gone into *ghaibah,* or seclusion, from whence he continued to preserve his followers in the true faith.

The intricacies of Shī'ah Islam in both these main segments are too complex to be disentangled here. There was, in its generative principle of immediacy, an instinctive tendency to sectarian division, as devotion or partisanship came to attach, competitively, to different figures in the sequence up to "concealment," and in the situation that followed it. The notion of "the hidden Imām" both necessitated and invited fissiparous tendencies wherever loyalties and emotions were finalized at competing points. The chronic sectarianism of Shī'ah Islam is seen by Sunnis as justifying the firm discipline of the Sunnī alternative, with its rejection of personal cults outside the final Prophet and its relative immunity thereby from the excesses and unpredictabilities of Shī'ah eschatology.

The emotional strength and cultic deviation of the Shī'ahs is most readily indicated by a study of their shrines, which through long periods asserted effective priority over Mecca itself. Pilgrimage as the unitary ritual in Islam became itself an instrument of separation. The concentric gave way to the eccentric. 'Alī's grave at Najaf; Karbalā' itself, both in Iraq; Mashhad in Persia, being the shrine of Imām Riḍā, as well as the burial place of the great Hārūn al-Rashīd; and the Kāẓimain in Baghdad, where Mūsā, seventh Imām and Muḥammad, ninth Imām, were buried, all became Shī'ah centers of devotion and the first three, in particular, powerful rivals of the orthodox *Ḥajj* itself. Political tensions and provincial passions also contributed, from time to time, to curtail or divert the classic pilgrimage. Though Shī'ahs have compelling religious reasons, through the Prophet and 'Alī and certain of the later Imāms, to hold faithfully to Mecca and Medina, the local loyalties as well as Sunnī enmities have often assured to Mashhad and Karbalā' and Najaf a more dominant devotion.

The Shī'ah divergence is equally striking in tradition, piety, and Quranic exegesis. The history of partisanship begat a partisanship about history. The controversies over succession and schism embittered the narratives. How "bad," for example, were the Umayyads? There was sharp contention, too, about the currency and credentials of the traditions, studied in Chapter 2, wherever these involved issues bearing on Sunnī-Shī'ah positions—which were, of course, numerous. Traditionalists were ranged in hostile camps.

The cleavage persisted likewise through the entire cultic life. *Ṣalāt* and its *Dhikr* were of necessity common to both. But the Shī'ah segment had its own patterns of mysticism and, as might be expected, developed by far the most esoteric forms. Aside from the *Tarīqahs,* Shī'ah piety showed itself far more receptive than Sunnī Islam to the influences of the environment, giving birth for example in early nineteenth century Persia to the cult of Bābism from which, in turn, Bahā'ism sprang.

Nowhere, however, was its characteristic energy more intense than in the genesis and persistence of the commemoration of the Passion of Ḥusain. The pathos and pain of this reenactment of the tragedy of Karbalā' have no parallel in Sunnī Islam. Through the centuries it has remained as a focus of emotion. The faithful mourn the fallen saint and relive the grim details of the tragic day when all but five of "the elect seed" and retinue perished, including the daughter of Ḥusain in her bridal array.

This drama of the tenth of Muḥarram gives moving voice to Shī'ah belief in the self-renouncing virtue of Ḥusain's death. Devotion sees him as the martyr at the hands of evil, who went to his death saying: "I have washed my hands of life; I have girded myself to do the will of God." Shī'ahs do not believe that he could have been so tragically a victim except by Divine foreknowledge. Clearly, then, he was an oblation for the cause of Islam and from his innocent sorrows redemption must flow for the community of faith. Pardon, mediation, virtue are to be found in the vicarious sacrifice which cruelty exacted—a cruelty that in its telling staggered with horror the whole Muslim world and in its recollection represents for all Shī'ahs the epitome of human crime.

Beyond these divergencies over history, authority, tradition, and cult, Shī'ah Muslims differ from Sunnis over the Qur'ān itself. The absence of 'Alī's name from it, and its silence about explicit Shī'ah claims, inspire the charge that it has been in places corrupted or adjusted by Sunnī hands. There are, it is alleged, at least two Surahs wanting which would have given the Shī'ahs comfort and confirmation. Ingenuity also can help to supply what is lacking by slight alterations to vary the sense, in forced and artificial ways which certainly command no support among Sunnis. With their concepts of the Imāms, Shī'ahs tend, further, to insist that all interpretation must be allegorical, requiring the special illumination that only the Imāms, or their spokesmen, the *mujtahids,* could attain. Ismailis, in particular, find every statement of the Qur'ān eluding direct or literal meaning and, therefore, out of the range of normal *tafsīr,* or commentary. More extreme forms of this attitude eliminate exegesis almost entirely, setting the Qur'ān totally within the secret purview of the hidden Imām. There is also the claim that the official text is relative to the original book which the hidden Imām will finally reveal.

Shī'ahs, in varying ways, read their sectarian interest where the text gives opportunity. Thus, for example, the familiar words in Surah 33:33. "People of the house (*Ahl al-Bait*), God only wills to put away from you all uncleanness and to cleanse you." The phrase "people of the house," usually understood as either Muḥammad's wives, or the denizens of the *Ka'bah* precincts, is taken by Shī'ah thought to refer to 'Alī, Fāṭimah and their family. The verse then becomes the ground for a doctrine of the immaculate Imāms. Passages which seem to indicate prophetic sinfulness are handled in such a way as to exclude that implication.

Despite the many legacies of estrangement, a will to rapprochement between Sunnis and Shī'ahs has been at work in recent years and much progress has been made. The abatement of fanaticism has contributed to this. In so far as Shī'ah allegiance belongs with national identity, whether Persian, Indian, East African, Yemeni, or the rest, modern conditions of interpenetration have served to allay its sharpness and to disqualify some of its more extreme forms of deviation.

Yet there is truth in the view that the abiding Sunnī-Shī'ah cleavage, deep as it is, relates to a common unity. It is a family quarrel. It concerns fundamental issues of authority and community which could not divide if they did not, in measure, unite. It witnesses to the intensity with which Islam registers ultimate problems of religion. Each segment exemplifies postures of faith and aspects of establishment that recur with comparable divisiveness in other creeds. For all their antipathy, they still express the *Ummah* they disrupt.

The *Ummah* theme may be assessed from quite a different angle by taking stock of the Islamic attitude to outsiders and its resulting theory of toleration. Paganism, polytheism, and atheism are repugnant to Islam and must be characterized as *Dār al-Ḥarb*—realms to be brought by *Jihād* under the authority of the true faith. From the outset the view was that the Caliphate and idolatry could not coexist. The latter must be eliminated.

But there were tolerated minorities, Jews and Christians, known as *dhimmis,* who were allowed to maintain their faith and worship within their own families. They were subjected to special taxation and suffered several disabilities, varying from time to time and place to place. The greatest was the prohibition of all external recruitment. Only those born Christians could be Christians, and likewise for Jews. It was assumed that the minorities would never receive adhesions from among Muslims. They enjoyed a freedom only to persist, not a freedom to baptize or to receive. It was thus a toleration ensuring freedom to remain but not a freedom to "become," except in one direction, namely into Islam. Since the Muslim was already there, he had no options. It was axiomatic that he should never seek to change. If he did, the law of apostasy forbade the notion and barred the way on pain of death and disinheritance. It was impossible to de-Islamize. Islam was a faith no Muslim was outwardly free to abandon. There is no more eloquent demonstration of the meaning of *Ummah* than this situation. It was a principle of irreversible and irreducible community continuity. Change of faith was equivalent to political treachery.

But the permitted minorities had the option of remaining as they were born, or of becoming Muslim. In the course of the centuries they accepted this account of themselves. Such a toleration was immensely better than open persecution. But it was existence in faith, by the sufferance of empire and authority properly and only wielded by the one faith, Islam. Those who embraced Islam were accepting religiously the sovereignty that had already acquired them politically. Those who held to their faith did so despite its complete political displacement. The notable position that individual Jews and Christians came to enjoy in the management of financial, educational or, in Ottoman days, military, aspects of the Caliphate, should not obscure the basic disabilities of their communities, since there were prudential or personal reasons for their functions. The legacies of *dhimmī* status remain to this day.[2] In its commendable toleration Islam never abandoned the axiom that it was made to rule.

That is the situation we must imaginatively understand if we are truly to take the measure of what happened to the *Ummah* in the nineteenth century. Here was an aberration indeed in the historical process; the whole flow of destiny turned bewilderingly out of its right course. Muslims, in large stretches of *Dār al-Islām,* found themselves under non-Muslim rule. Western empire came, dislodging and subduing Islamic sovereignties; and Muslim subjects became, so to speak, *dhimmis* in their own lands, religiously tolerated but politically subservient. Only Turkey, Arabia, Iran and Afghanistan, among Muslim lands, were able to elude in form, if not always in effect, the political mastery of the West. The British Raj in India and the Dutch Empire in what is now Indonesia were the largest and longest of these alien dominions over Islam. The story in the Arab East is briefer but also more bitter. Algeria was conquered by France finally in 1848, Tunis was annexed in 1883, and Morocco occupied from 1912. Britain established its protectorate in Egypt in 1882 and, with the French, shared the Arab lands of the eastern Mediterranean in the post-1918 mandates that replaced the Ottoman Empire. Russia, too, seized control of various Islamic Khanates in Central Asia between the seventeenth and the nineteenth centuries. In Africa, Europe similarly alienated Muslim power from Muslim rulers, in varying ways, until within the last decade. The *Ummah* of Islam was apoliticized (if the term is allowed). Muslims were governed instead of governing.

This reversal of authentic existence created a most painful and desolating dilemma. Did *Dār al-Islām* still exist where British, French or Dutch authority prevailed?

We can conveniently take the measure of that question by reference to the post-1857 situation within Indian Islam, remembering that the same searching of heart was entailed in every other place and period until counterimperialism ended it. The Indian War of Independence, or the Indian Mutiny (depending on where you read your history)—being premature, impetuous, and abortive—resulted only in entrenching the British Raj more firmly. In its aftermath, Muslims, who had played the major part, fell into even deeper frustration than the Hindus. Their cause seemed indeed bleak. The great Mughal power was finally and miserably extinct. Clearly Muslims were no longer in *Dār al-Islām*—the more obviously so by the sorry failure of their struggle. To be sure, the mosques were open, Ramaḍān and pilgrimage were feasible, Muslim personal law was enforced, and prayer was free to be made. By all these criteria Islam was in true being. But were these the sole criteria? Manifestly not.

Although the regime was, on its own conditions, benign and uncorrupt, it was British not Indian, Victorian not Mughal, "Christian" not Islamic. The old glories of Akbar and Aurangzeb were departed. Muslims, by political measure, were in a sort of *Dār al-Ḥarb,* a territory needing to be liberated, though their own homeland. Their history had entered something like an exile from a true destiny, without any physical disruption. It contradicted the whole pattern of Islamic assumption, requiring Muslims to see in Islam "just a religion," independent of, indeed immune from, the external political realities. Such a requirement Islam had never before faced, willingly, or on so large a scale, or in so seemingly permanent a prospect. In post-1857 India the British Raj seemed set for an interminable stay.

The majority of Muslims were sullenly minded to deplore their adversity and to find a dubious solace in apathy and dismay, holding their political hopelessness to be a total tragedy. One of their leaders, Sayyid Aḥmad Khān, (1817–1898 A.D.) read the omens in a different way. He emerged at this time as the vigorous exponent of activism and a progressive philosophy. He became one of the pioneer modernists in Indian Islam. He was ready to argue that *Dār al-Islām* still existed in India by virtue of the religious institutions and to urge, further, that Muslims must embrace and welcome the norms and outlook of their overlords. He set himself to interpret Islam to the West and the West to Islam. His travels in Europe and England had made him, perhaps excessively, Anglophile and pro-Western. He founded at Aligarh the Muhammadan College to foster modern education and train a Muslim leadership ready for initiative. Whether in their Hindu or their British relationships, Muslims, he contended, were well advised to equip themselves by scholarship and science for the developing future. It was pointless to repine and wait abjectly for days of Mughal splendor to return.

Aḥmad Khān's mission served a purpose, but the future lay with a more assertive style of nationalism. Before his death he came himself to modify somewhat the exuberance of his confidence in imitation of the culture of the West. Independence in the familiar twentieth century sense undoubtedly represented the ultimate psychological and practical prerequisite for true identity and self-responsibility in the subcontinent. To that extent the sentiment that said: "The British presence makes us virtually *Dār al-Ḥarb*" was right. Much of Aḥmad Khān's writing now looks oddly out of line with the assumptions dominating the last half century. Nevertheless, his efforts contributed much to generate the energies and capacities by which political criteria of what it takes to be fully Muslim became again dominant and successful.

The point of his significance here is that he negotiated a sharp historical crisis within the *Ummah* concept. It was able, as a result, both to weather and surmount the circumstances that conspired to make Islam only "religious," and so to persist, however painfully, without statehood and ultimately to repossess it, in one twentieth century form or another.

The interim between the loss of political power and its recovery was, of course, considerably shorter in the Arab world than in India or Indonesia. But, longer or shorter, the experience taught Islam in hard terms both the possibility and the incongruity of existing without sanction of governing power. The lesson of that abeyance has contributed much to contemporary attitudes within Islam. Though *Dār al-Islām,* without the Caliphate, is again politically in being, it is a radically transformed concept and, because of secularization, can no longer be applied with the old simplicity. Once again politically sustained, the *Ummah* is facing stresses for its form and spirit from the modern world, more taxing even than imperialism. But these stresses have to do with the abiding problems of unity and diversity, of universality and identity, that have always characterized the house of Islam. Those twin themes, both in retrospect and prospect, will occupy the final chapter of our study.

Islamic community, to conclude, is thus intimately related to the major elements of human existence, with birth, nation, and state. For all but the entering convert, it has the sanction of birth. The Muslim is so born and participates by continuity of kindred rather than crisis of decision. It is assumed that to be born is to belong. The new adherent originates a like tradition by his adoption of the faith. Yet the *Ummah* is not an ethnic concept. For it is open to all mankind and has never circumscribed its message in an elect or private people. It contrives to accept and harness any nationalism. Being Islamic is constitutive of numerous nation-states, but without serious embarrassment to its multinational capacities. To some purer thinkers, or thinkers in their loftier moments, nationalism is a dubious, and perhaps temporary, compromise of the pan-Islamic consciousness. But, in the main, the *Ummah* contains nations without losing itself. It likewise serves and recruits the state, through whatever diverse forms and theories. It means to render to God and to Caesar without isolating one direction of duty from the other. It persists through, and with, a quite fundamental schism in its own being, and it has successfully survived the termination of its most symbolic institution.

In all these ways what Muḥammad inaugurated lives and moves with the basic human realities. It is there with its multitudes, in their begetting, their belonging, their governing and their worshipping, through all the many places of their habitation both of time and territory.

Some Questions

1. How does the Sunnī/Shī'ah divergence within Islam illustrate basic problems of religion in respect of authority, history, and devotion?

2. What was the Caliphate? What is the significance of its termination?

3. Explain and evaluate the assumptions underlying the Islamic concept of toleration and the recognition of minorities.

4. How and why does the Islamic understanding of the *Ummah* differ from "chosen people," "church," "denomination," and "religious community"? Out of what historical factors was it developed?

5. Explain the nature of the problem created for Islam by Western imperialism.

7. Questions of Time

"When the help of God comes and victory, and you see men thronging into the religion of God," says Surah 110, "then give glory to your Lord and seek His forgiveness." The passage is no doubt a warning of the crisis implicit in success, the different dangers of the breakthrough beyond the travail. But does it not imply more than a hint of the larger problems of the world and time, of widening spheres and lengthening years?

The suggestion, in this final chapter, is to consider with a very few examples the broad questions of time as they belong with Islam. The foregoing has left little occasion for history in its own right, and we cannot hope here to make this good. But history in the twentieth century has become acutely exacting. Things latent before have acquired a sharp urgency now and demand a more conscious reckoning than the past has given them.

They can be seen as in fact twin aspects of one theme—the relation of the faith to the rest of the world and to the sequence of the centuries. Islam was never understood to be secluded, private, or ethnically exclusive, and it certainly demanded to make good its finality in a steady perpetuity. But to be set for the ends of the earth and the rest of time is to incur the accumulating and perennial issues of place and age.

After noting the firm quality of Islam as a race-transcending religion, we turn to capture the current dimensions of the issue with the help of a recent novel from within African Islam, namely, *L'Aventure Ambiguë*, by[1] Hamidou Kane, to be discussed in detail below. Its author has a lively awareness of the tensions experienced by a traditional believer in his encounter with secular men and with the modern, human autonomy in its rejection of the Divine.

The bearings of Islam with the rest of the world, however, looked very different five hundred years earlier. After Hamidou Kane and his Senegalese perplexities we turn back, in this chapter, to the celebrated Ibn Khaldūn in the fourteenth century. He may be taken as the supreme exponent of questions of time, in the whole sequence of Islamic thought. Though he lived in the midst of political changes that closely affected his own fortunes, he was able to make his assessments of Islam from a position of theological assurance and dogmatic confidence. His theory of history has a power of perception and a range of vision of truly classic quality, and his interpretation exemplifies the Muslim virtues of integrity, realism, and sympathy.

Of a different temper, again, are the illuminating characteristics of the Wahhābī movement, to which we pass for a third perspective of enquiry into Islam and time. Beginning in eighteenth century Arabia and having a vigorous twentieth century career, Wahhābism represents the attitudes of conservatism, of suspicion and fear, of self-sufficiency and militant defiance of change. It is all the more telling an example for the fact of its encounter with a most concentrated form of modern technology developing the oil wealth beneath its desert sands.

Wahhābism understood original Islam as a once-for-all perfection, related to all ensuing time in fixed and uncompromising terms, and it proceeded on the Islamic instinct that the state is the surest and the most proper instrument of faith. Contemporary Islamic nationalism presents many evidences, in different temper, of that second conviction, but pursues it with very contrasted ideals of religious meaning and establishment. We have opportunity only for the briefest notice in conclusion of aspects of that postimperial renewal of Islamic independence with which we began in the introductory quotation from President 'Abd al-Nāṣir of Egypt. There are cogent reasons here for a concentration on the issues of the state and of modernity as they are found within Indian Islam. India, with its Muslim minority, and Pakistan, with its Islamic state, represent the two shapes of modern destiny, and within them lie the perennial questions about time and the faith.

But even this concluding picture must be allowed a final postscript. The ultimate *religious* problem of history is surely that of suffering and evil. From these, contemporary Muslims have borne much in recent history. It is perhaps fitting then to leave the last word with one who may be described as the most articulate sufferer in all Arabic literature.

All these representatives of "questions of time" take their place, diversely, within the human unity of Islam. Its universality, it is true, was in genesis Arab and Arabic and Arabian. It had a revelatory language and a native ground. It could not have been otherwise. For history can never receive or attain a universal except through a particular. Islam derives from these natal characteristics. It belongs irreversibly with a man from among the Quraish, a book in the speech of Mecca, and an expansion from the wells of Arabian history. Even the imagery of the Qur'ān, its vision of heaven and hell, live in these accidents of place and climate.

So inaugurated, however, it seeks and intends the world. The Arabic Scripture has a humanity to educate. The Arab messenger is sent, via his twin cities, to the entire earth. The rule of Islam kept his lineage but enclosed a far diversity of language, land, and life. His native tongue remains peculiarly related to the word from heaven, but addresses every speech. Revelation is, at once, untranslatable and missionary, uniquely the Arabs' but inclusively everybody's.

So characterized and determined, what may the faith or the community be, and not be, become and not become, hold and not hold, in order to be consistently itself, through changes of context and of century? There were Meccan emigrants and Medinan "aiders" in the *Hijrah* itself. What of the originators and recruits, the old hands and the newcomers, in all the migrations of Islam?

One point can be made firmly at once. Islam has achieved a remarkable degree of interracial tolerance and coexistence. It is more effectively ecumenical in human terms than Christianity and has no place for the privacies among humanity of traditional Jewry. Its tensions have been religious or political, rather than racial, even where, as with the tragic sufferings of Armenians at the hands of Turks, or betwixt Muslims and Hindus, it seems to be otherwise. Those who invoke Islam in behalf of racial hatred, or *apartheid,* or in the name of Black Power, are either ignorantly or wilfully prostituting Islam. It was pilgrimage to Mecca which served to disabuse the Negro leader, Malcolm X, of this misinterpretation in 1964. Before that experience he had seen Islam as an instrument of Black Power *against* the white world. His testimony is a moving tribute to the capacity, both of the pilgrimage in particular, and of Islam in general, to exemplify and make actual a genuine transcendence of racial passions and enmities.[2] Muslim writers are proud to remind their readers that the first muezzin, calling to prayer, was Bilāl, an Ethiopian, who used to pray devoutly as he did so for the turning of the hostile Quraish. His country, African and Christian, was the first to give sanctuary to Muḥammad's persecuted followers, fugitive from Mecca.

It needs to be remembered, in this context, that Islam has never been related to the rest of mankind with the sort of cultural advantage and prolonged preponderance of externally based power that have characterized the impact of Western empire. There has been no equal in all history to the exploitative opportunity of the West over the rest of the world in the nineteenth century. Islam had its own versions of imperialism, swift, decisive, and then assimilative and for the most part permanent. In its African forms, whether Almoravid or Fulānī in the West, Arab, Yao, and the like in the East, Islamic penetration, though martial and vigorous, did not leave the kind of legacies that remain from Western imperialism, with its pride of aloofness, its disruptive technology, and its material superiority. Islam's militant relationships have been in the encounter of religions, rather than the stresses of race. Its *Jihād* is on behalf of faith against faiths: peoples are no more than the arena of the other struggle.

But is it also, in that arena of peoples, a *Jihād* of faith against change? Nowhere, in recent Muslim writing, has the force of the question been more pointedly stated than in the novel of the Senegalese Shaikh Hamidou Kane: *L'Aventure Ambiguë,* published in 1962, when the author was thirty-three. Against a strongly autobiographical background, it sets down the tension between traditional Islamic religion and the patterns and assumptions of Western civilization. The hero, Samba Diallo, like the author, spends his early years in the Quranic school and a strictly Muslim home. Thierno, called "the Master" in the novel, is his schoolmaster mentor in the teachings of the Qur'ān, from whom Samba learns a total piety. But his aunt, sister of the chief of the Diallobé people, senses the threat to faith and morals implicit in European influence and power. She recommends that Samba, as the chief's nephew, be sent to France to become familiar with the new ways, as a necessary defense against their mastery—a defense which ignorance can only undermine. Unlike some other African stories, *L'Aventure Ambiguë* suggests no inherent *human* inferiority of the African to the European, but writes of both in equal terms. The sense of the "advantage" of Western technology implies no essential superiority. This dignity of identity only makes the inner problem the more acute and vivid.

Samba, like his author, goes first to the French school in Senegal and then on to Paris. There he slowly loses his Islamic faith. With a remarkable clarity and forcefulness of style, Hamidou Kane traces this gradual but somehow inevitable sequence and paints its course in a series of sharp contrasts, between the edge of the Sahara and the deep, Senegal mysteries of nature and, on the other side, the busy boulevards, the logical intellects, the cold precision of the Parisian society, in and out of the university. The ardent, intense, sometimes ecstatic, Muslim religion that he describes among the Diallobé people is symbolized in "the Master," a figure at once venerable and gallant, with a spirituality rooted in the Qur'ān's sacramental view of "the signs of God," and nourished by the sincerest practice of *Dhikr.*

Samba's letters home betray the steady erosion of his beliefs, despite his wistful sense of their preciousness, and his perceptive disquiet about the pervasive materialism and the rational brilliance of his French friends, among whom are some expatriate Africans whose hybrid cultural confusion only sharpens his dilemmas. It is the honesty of the inner tension, skillfully conveyed by the author, that gives the story its authentic quality. Samba, critical of both worlds, is torn by the alienation he feels within himself, by the sense of compromise, and yet of inevitability, in his loss of faith. The author's sustained concentration on the spiritual and philosophical issues to the exclusion of matters political and social, which, inviting to activism, or to emotion, are normally an emotional relief and a happy mental confusion in such stories and encounters, only serves to make the climax the more compelling. Samba cannot be both Muslim and materialist, Diallobé and Parisian. But he cannot be either in repudiation of the other. He is an ambiguous unity in dichotomy.

Summoned home by his father who is disquieted by the drift of his letters, Samba loyally returns. But the old faith cannot be regained. "The Master" dies and another character, "the Fool," assumes the rôle of guardian of the old order. But having rejected all modernity as a falsehood, he is a traditionalist of the most negative kind. The climax of tragedy and loneliness comes when Samba is killed by "the Fool," because he cannot bring himself to pray at "the Master's" grave. The whole is a moving study of the stresses, indeed of the irreconcilabilities, between the two worlds, and within those of whom time makes a generation in crisis. Its pathos is the more full, in that the lost world was so authentically aware, in its *islām,* of the mysteries without which man, for all his sophistication, remains a stranger from the glory.

L'Aventure Ambiguë is Hamidou Kane's first novel. Its hero has no Senegalese precedents. He carries in his own person the whole brunt of the conflict. It is this which explains the tragic conclusion. But this losing battle does not rightly argue a lost cause. On the contrary, the ambiguous adventure goes on. Indeed, in a manifold sense it has been perpetual, through the differing equations of history. The purpose of citing the novel at some length is to gather the underlying themes with the peculiar force that the twentieth century imparts.

Relation to the universal and the external could be attained with far less anxiety or peril when Islam was outwardly in command of its world. There is no example of that sort more to the point than the work of Ibn Khaldūn, the most outstanding theorist of history ever to emerge from within Islam. He lived through acute, if sometimes petty, interior crises in North African and Spanish Muslim politics, but thought and wrote from a firm and unshaken assurance about the universal validity of Islamic dogma. From that double circumstance, of flux and of solidity, he undertook to assess the whole panorama of human existence in time and place. The result was a monumental sociology of history which continues to fascinate twentieth century historiography. Even the briefest notice of Ibn Khaldūn can serve our current questions well.

His great classic. *Al-Muqaddimah,*[3] formed the Introduction to his *History of the Berber Peoples* and occupied more than fifty years of reflection, scholarship, and composition—years which were passed in vexing insecurities both of life and fortune. Born in Tunis in 1332, Ibn Khaldūn died in Cairo in 1406. In successive stages of his career we find him in Fez, Biskra, Tlemcen, Bougie, and Taughẓūt, towns of North Africa, and in Granada, Cairo, Damascus, and Alexandria. He spent five years, in the thirteen-eighties, on a pilgrimage to Mecca, and later lost both family and goods in shipwreck. He knew the ups and downs of the diplomat and court secretary and forsook them in the second half of his life for the quieter fields of teaching. But, serving also as a *qāḍī,* or court-judge, he was dogged by dangers to the end. There was, therefore, a deeply existential quality about his interrogation of history, developed grimly in the tumult of affairs. It is noteworthy that what he achieved was not so much a *philosophy* of history in the strict sense—a proceeding requiring a much greater quality of curiosity than his dogmatic commitment allowed, but rather a study of the circumstances of historical flux, a sociology, an analysis of the life-cycle of states, of the rise and fall of empires, of the bearing of climate, habitat and race on the patterns of culture and the survival power of institutions. His was a practical, rather than a speculative, index to the nature of human history, a geography of politics, as genius and Islamic instincts in partnership could set them down. He was, in fact, less successful in actual narrative than in the elucidation of general perspectives.

He was thus profoundly interested in a whole humanity outside Islam. He was, so to speak, engaging in external relations, taking stock of other existences in the stream of history. He was implicitly involved in the question whether Islam, or any other faith and culture, is really self-sufficient, whether what is absolutely believed is ever consciously in debt. But he broached these issues only at a tangent. His whole stance was determined by a clear insistence on the finality of Islam. Revelation meant for him a disallowance of rationality, except in corroboration of dogmas accepted in their own revealed right. "We must believe and know," he wrote, "what we have been commanded to believe and know." "We must not seek to prove its correctness rationally, even if rational intelligence contradicts it." All that must be left to God through the Prophet, as the supreme Lawgiver.[4]

He conceded that external philosophy had attracted Muslim thinkers in the preceding centuries and that scholastic controversy with heretics had also imported an element of speculation into Islam. For necessarily, impugning authority as it does, heresy tempts the defense of faith into reliance on intellect. This he feared and deplored. Even Plato, he noted, had ended in uncertainties about the Divine. "If after all the trouble and toil, we find only conjectures, the conjectures we had at the beginning may as well suffice us."

Thus his wide-ranging sociology proceeded by the sanction, and within the premises, of a dogmatic theology which he took wholly on trust and trusted wholly. The sense of Islam as culminatory excited the search for a pattern in historical time. But the sense of it as final dictated a prejudgment about what the study of history must be expected to do, namely to illustrate God's dealings, confirm the moral order, attest the Qur'ān, and edify the faithful. But even with these presuppositions, he accomplished an immense task in the study of social factors in history and found solace from the vagaries of his own misfortunes. His belief is creation, providence, and the seal of prophethood in Muḥammad both inspired and circumscribed his motive concepts. He attained a massive expression of inclusive sympathies, but did so from a full Islamic self-sufficiency.

It is necessary to remember that he lived in the wake of great upheavals in *Dār al-Islām,* and that, from the time of the renowned Al-Ghazālī, a strong suspicion of intellectualism had settled down upon the Muslim spirit. The notable theologians of the tenth and eleventh centuries had shown a livelier readiness for reason and did in fact play an important role as transmitters to the modern west of the Greek experience of philosophy.

It would seem a quite arbitrary transition, a random move, to pass from fourteenth century Tunis and Cairo to eighteenth century Arabia, from Ibn Khaldūn to Muḥammad ibn 'Abd al-Wahhāb. But Wahhābism is a no less useful crux in the dual problem of the universal and the loyal. It arises, it is true, as a sharp antagonism within the faith, as an internal rebellion against Muslim decline. But, as such, it provides inspiration and pattern for twentieth century conservatism against external stresses and alien inroads. Also it brings us close to insistent contemporary issues by the irony of its geographical home in Arabia having become the scene of the most concentrated invasion of technological change in the entire Islamic world.

In genesis, however Wahhābism was wholly an internal phenomenon. Its founder was 'Abd al-Wahhāb (1704–1792), a native of Najd in Central Arabia. He belonged to the Ḥanbalī school, strictest of the four canonical schools of law, and he espoused the rigorism of the redoutable Ibn Taimiyyah (d. 1328), who disallowed all innovation, pilgrimages to shrines, saint worship, the cult of intercession, and other accretions. 'Abd al-Wahhāb established a powerful, personal ascendancy over his followers, for whom he was simply "the shaikh." He demanded a return to the unadulterated Islam of the Prophet and the Qur'ān. He considered that the Arabia of his own day was in *Jāhiliyyah,* "ignorance," no less than in the seventh century, and he proposed to fight it in the manner of Muḥammad himself, by a crusading zeal for "unitarianism," the name by which his movement was known. *Ijmā'* he limited to the first three centuries of Islam. He firmly closed the door on *Ijtihād.* He laid absolute stress on the Divine unity and held that the Divine will was totally unobligated to any principle or law of being. Those within Islam contravening his puritan severities he classed as polytheists. He forbade the use of the rosary and the traditional ceremonies, or *maulids,* in honor of Muḥammad's birthday.

In the enforcement of his system he relied heavily on the ruler, whose essential function was to apply the rigor of the *Sharī'ah* and embrace *Jihād* in Wahhābī terms. It was thus that there emerged the formidable alliance of the unitarian reformers and the house of Sa'ūd, which, beginning in the mid eighteenth century, has endured to our own day. The Sa'ūdis gave political occasion and military success to the dogmatists and reaped, in turn, the fruits of their fiery ardor and will to battle. The first dramatic successes came in the first decade of the nineteenth century, when the twin sanctuaries of Mecca and Medina were occupied and Wahhābī dominion stretched across most of the Arabian peninsula and up to the gates of Damascus. In 1801, Karbalā' was sacked and Mecca, in 1806, purged of practices repugnant to its zealot masters. These indignities aroused the Ottoman Turks, who, through Muḥammad 'Alī of Egypt, regained suzerainty in 1818. Wahhābī fortunes ebbed, then flowed again, only to ebb again through the nineteenth century. But in 1902 began their steady return to total ascendancy, through the genius and prowess of 'Abd al-'Azīz ibn Sa'ūd (d. 1953), the great architect of their modern destiny. Both in success and failure, Wahhābism renewed the several qualities which had characterized original Islam. It came near to being what its own ideal demanded, namely the seventh century made actual again. It did so in large measure by the same criteria—energy, nomadism allied with faith, Arabism in religious tide, a politico-dogmatic unity, and a militancy in the name of the one God. The Sa'ūdī/Wahhābī partnership might even have renewed the wider achievements of initial Islam, but for the paradox of its fortunes in the discovery of oil. Here was a more subtle and ambiguous force than the seventh century had ever faced, surreptitiously maturing in the Arabian hearthland itself and conspiring with its very sands against the ancient order of the faith, at least as Wahhābism received it.

Oil was first discovered in eastern Arabia in 1938. It was massively exploited only after 1945. But it ended an immunity almost sacrosanct since before Muḥammad, an immunity, geographical and economic, from the empires of the outside world, and from alien disruptions of the soul. Portents of that transformation, it is true, had been gathering. The first newspaper had appeared in 1924 and the radio soon after. But it was oil that was decisive, both in the corrosion of the traditional world and in the material means to the construction of a new order of things. Wahhābī Islam has only slowly acceded to this silent and continuing revolution. It has departed from a strictly literal *Sharī'ah* in the 1962 abolition of slavery, and in other ways. Its partnership of more than two centuries with the Sa'ūdī state, with the Imamate, and later the kingship, of the house of Sa'ūd, has been overtaken by developments from without which the latter can well digest and command but which are highly disconcerting to its own militant simplicity. These are the end of nomadism, the penetrations of the West, the works of technology and the secularizing wealth. Unlike the earlier troughs of Wahhābī fortune after 1818 and before Ibn Sa'ūd, all things now conspire, even geology itself, against a renewal of the seventh century.

Wahhābī unitarianism, nevertheless, has set the theme and the temper for the zealot instinct in modern Islam. The Sanūsiyyah in Libya represent a comparable hegemony of ruler and religion, though in a realm geographically less insulated than Arabia. By its assertion of Arabism against Ottoman dominion, Wahhābism may be seen as anticipating the much later Arab nationalisms in the Middle East. It had no scruples about having to direct its revolt against another Muslim community. Thus the thesis of Islamic disqualification of other Muslims, which it sustained with such vehemence, is one we find recurring, distressfully and stridently, through all contemporary Muslim life.

It found echo also, remarkably, in various parallel movements in Indian Islam, for which Wahhābism seems to have held considerable fascination. Shāh Wāli Ullāh (1703–1765), though independently a leader of Islamic revival in Delhi, was filled with veneration for Arabia as a kind of true homeland of Islam. He appealed to original Arab ways and to Arabic in his defense against Indian or Persian elements which he counted responsible for Islamic decline. Wahhābism, as it were, vindicated this attitude; and later, more militantly puritan sects such as the Ahl-i-Qur'ān and the Baraidī perpetuated a Wahhābī impulse in the subcontinent. Pilgrimage to Mecca fostered the kinship of temper. The approximate identity of interest and the bond it created makes a significant contrast with the more general pattern of relative intellectual isolation of Muslim peoples from each other in the eighteenth and early nineteenth centuries.

The legatees of Wahhābism today outside Arabia are, in broad terms, the Muslim Brotherhood in Egypt and the Jamā'at-i-Islāmī in Pakistan, and their counterparts elsewhere. The former, founded in the nineteen-thirties, by Ḥasan al-Bannā' (1906–1949), aims to rid Islam of moral and doctrinal compromise and to renew its pristine zeal. It differs from Wahhābism in its firm subordination of the "national" element to its view of *Dār al-Islām* as a single Islamic community. It has never been successful in welding this cause to political power. It is also abreast, in study and policy, of the modern world and sees the Qur'ān as yielding effective direction for the economic and social problems it presents. It has a demanding sense of urgency and makes exacting claims upon its membership. Yet it oversimplifies the meaning of *islām* and, for all its energy, foreshortens the task of religious apologetic and of moral guidance in the contemporary situation.

In the political field these conservative elements, for the most part, have met a frustration which has tempted some of them into subversive attitudes. Yet they stand for a view of Islam which sees the faith as properly determining what the world shall be, rather than the world the faith. In their scheme of disciplines, the Wahhābis provided the *mutawwiʿ*—"the obedience-maker." He was responsible for enforcing an undeviating conformity. Sadly, the modern world does not recognize his office, and human nature is an ancient evader. "Obedience-dreamers" perhaps, or schemers; but no more.

This intractability of the human world to the religious ideal seems to many Muslims today to require a more modest philosophy about the actualization of Islam in the contemporary world—a philosophy which invokes the same Wahhābī concept of the ruler as instrument, but does so in quite contrasted fashion. Realist enough to refrain from the notion of being an "obedience-maker," it adopts instead what may loosely be described as the role of an "obedience-context." It undertakes to provide a political setting, a power framework, for whatever religious and intellectual forces may be able to achieve of Islamic ideology, consistent with the requirements of the power itself. It affords an overall "umbrella" of recovered political authority under which, however diversely and perhaps remotely, Islam may exist and fulfill itself.

We have noted in the Introduction and in earlier chapters the implicit necessity of power to doctrine, of ruler to prophet, of state to faith, in traditional Islam. We have also pondered the deep and burdensome aberration from the proper pattern which Islamic history underwent in the years of Western empire. It was, therefore, natural that the energies making for independence should have revived, and been revived by, this confidence in the political dimension. This leaves loyalty a much more open question, and universality a more doubtful one.

The most dramatic and conspicuous of many examples is undoubtedly Pakistan, inasmuch as its creation involved a costly partition and transformed the concept of religious communalism (obtaining in British India) into the concept of separate nationalisms. The illogicality here was that the nation-state theory for the majority Muslim areas consigned the minority Muslims to *final* communalism in their areas. This necessity, unavoidable as it was, only underlines the determination behind the nation-state idea. The conviction that Muslims are not properly so without an Islamic state of their own is the more evidently insistent for having to be cruelly selective. Much in preimperial India no doubt sustains that decision. But federal unity was a viable option which would have kept all the subcontinent's Muslims together, though only at the price of political coexistence and numerical inferiority.

The *apologia* for Pakistan is, therefore, an important index to our double concern about the universal and the valid. But it is also an ambiguous index. For the demand for the all important Islamic state drew into a single policy for its acquisition a wide variety of views. The great architect of the new state, Muḥammad 'Alī Jinnah (1876–1948) seems to have regarded religion as simply a potent state-maker and to have been content with an "obedience-context" in the barest sense. His remarkable acumen and astute opportunism saw and embraced the demand for statehood as its own emotional right. Common folk were enthusiastic. Ultraconservatives and strong radicals could share the policy *for* the state, while differing sharply about their anticipations of how it would, or should, define itself in the end. Controversy and definition could be shelved while all concentrated, whatever their misgivings or incompatibilities, on the task of securing the prize.

These unified, but disparate, elements required to take a hand in characterizing the state once it was achieved. A whole decade of constitutional debate ensued (1947–1958 A.D.), culminating in a constitution which was, however, abrogated before it was inaugurated. The ensuing military régime since 1958 has had the same essential problem of the definition of Islam. One of the crucial ideas here is that of "repugnancy" to the Qur'ān. But there are several ways in which this might be determined: councils of *'ulamā',* the good sense of Muslim legislatures, the pervasive democracy of a Muslim population, or a constitutional organ of delay and revision over "doubtful" legislation. One obvious issue within these means to the truly Islamic is whether they are viable or feasible in modern conditions, and how, if so, they might suffice either purists or progressives. For it is clear that the Sambas of life's ambiguous adventure everywhere are not recalled to a static society from alien education. The equivalents of Hamidou Kane's Senegal and Paris are found inside all borders, and the Sambas, too, are becoming fathers in their turn. Men can no more grapple with universal problems in the particular assurance of Islam that Ibn Khaldūn enjoyed.

What, therefore, most Muslim governments propose today, having abandoned Wahhābī ideals of a forceful *Sharī'ah,* is to let a general, and variable, Islamic character suffice and, consistently with their political necessities, to let such factors as may occupy themselves with the interpretation and the conformity of the faith. But through them all, even Turkey, where secular, laïc revolution has gone furthest, and Tunis, where the leadership is most forthrightly modern, there is in varying form the conviction that somehow the Islamic way is embodied and made good, simply in that the imperial aliens are gone, and Muslims are back in, and with, power. There is, however, no clear consensus as to how that power, apart from being *ipso facto* Islam, should direct or achieve the religion. In Turkey, of course, aliens did not have to depart, for, except the Greeks briefly, they were not there. But the Ottoman Empire has gone, and the vigorous national state has returned to some degree of religious relevance.

This variable, but significant, statehood-Islam, representing both decision and ambiguity, is not available as a solution for those Muslims who live as minorities in other peoples' states, notably the Muslims of post-1947 India, and of the U.S.S.R. and—far fewer, but peculiarly significant—the Arab Muslims in Israel, now strangers in their own home.

All these, of course, lack what by Pakistanī criteria is the indispensable condition of authentic and sure survival, namely separate statehood. The Indian Muslim reaction to this exacting destiny is, therefore, an index to contemporary Muslim possibilities of a quite other character than those of statehood fulfillment. On the one hand there is the ever-present, progressive danger of assimilation to Hinduism. Argument for Pakistan perhaps remembered that even the great Akbar, chief architect of the mighty Mughal dynasty in the sixteenth century, became syncretistic towards Hinduism and ended by renouncing Islam for a new *Dīn-i-Ilāhī,* or "Divine" religion, of his own devising. If such perversion could occur from a throne of autocracy, what may minority inferiority not produce? An emperor's idiosyncrasies, of course, are not necessarily a precedent for a community's evolution.

But the questions are certainly exacting. Will the necessity to subsist permanently without statehood of their own evoke a more virile religious expression of Islam from Indian Muslims? Or will majority pressures, exerting themselves in countless ways even within a secular order, attenuate and enfeeble the Islamic will? Or will there be a new articulation of Islam, responding to new criteria of its essentials? These issues cannot yet be reported in detail. There are writers, such as Himāyūn Kabīr and A.A.A. Fyzee, giving creative Muslim thought to Hindu relationships. There is, too, the legacy of the leading Muslim Indian figure of the partition struggle, Abū-l-Kalām Āzād (1888–1958), statesman, exegete, and thinker, who abjured the whole policy of Muslim separatism and served with distinction in the creation and expression of the secular state in India. He wrote on Islam and the Qur'ān with a spiritual insight and commitment that are strangely absent from much of the apologia for Pakistan. Muḥammad 'Alī Jinnah left no Quranic commentary and no "diary of the heart" to posterity. Those of Āzād breathed a deep intensity and a lively independence of mind. He sought the essence of religion in "faith and right dealing," which he took to be the real *fiṭrah,* or spiritual quality, of original Islam. This he saw as having a unitary effect among men of good will across religious boundaries. It was the institutional forms of religion that proved divisive, both within faiths and between them.

The fearful and the dogmatists find this a sure prescription for error and compromise. Yet it remains an expression of the problem of universality we are discussing. Can faiths have relationships only on their own terms and from their own entrenchments of dogma or establishment? Yet can they *not* have them, if they inhabit common worlds with others and if they make claim to inclusive mission and universal truth? Indian Islam has at least the merit of knowing these problems in its own crises, impeded as it is by many deterrents of circumstance in rising to their demands.

While, further, it may choose to be introverted and "parochial," its very lack of Islamic statehood can save it from the ambiguity that a unitary nationalism, like that currently prevailing in Islam, involves for a universal religion. We have earlier noted the problem that political fragmentation sets in parting Muslims from Muslims. Minority Muslims do not have the comfort, or the alibi, of the state as an "obedience context," but their very exposure can constitute a deeper challenge to obedience.

A quite different form of this problem of the contemporary "religious" life of Islam obtains in present day Turkey. There the population is overwhelmingly Muslim and the state stands in full Turkish virility. But by action of that very statehood under the great Ataturk (1881–1938) Turkish Islam underwent a quite thoroughgoing secularization in the nineteen-twenties, with the Europeanization of law, the abolition of the religious endowments, the proscription of the Sufi Orders, and the complete official abeyance of all religious education for a whole generation. These measures were part of the recovery, modernization and "laïcization" of Turkey after the demise of Ottoman power in 1918. They constitute the most radical attack on establishment Islam ever to be generated from within a Muslim society.

The modification of these immense changes, with the political developments of the nineteen-fifties, has given new opportunity to Turkish Islam which has survived its chastenings and demonstrates renewed vitality. But history cannot be reversed and what is still at stake is the temper and form of Islamic faith, doctrine, and devotion within a nation ready, it would seem, for the values of religion but not for its tyrannies.

Pondering, in these ways, the yesterday and the morrow of contemporary Islam, two final questions remain. It often occurs to the sympathetic observer to enquire whether Muslims are ever in doubt, not, of course, about the periphery of events, for these are always precarious, but about the core of conviction. A recurrent phrase in the Qur'ān describes it as "a book in which there is no doubtfulness." To be free from *raibah* means a quality that obviates and dispels misgiving about itself. Ignorance, the *Jāhiliyyah,* is overcome by revelation. There is an assuring finality about the faith. Islam is religion perfected and to succeed is its proper destiny. Has it, then, any real room, as it were, for a loyal scepticism? Has it ever produced any great doubters from within, any genuine iconoclasts against itself? If not, how does it relate to the contemporary situation, where, almost of necessity, religious faith must learn to comprise not only itself but the doubt of itself, and wrestle patiently with the urge of some to say: "Lord, I believe; help Thou my unbelief." Islam has been, traditionally, impatient with the dubious and rigorous against apostacy. Whenever this is so there is a great unexaminedness about belief, a conspiracy of silence about latent, haunting questions.

Akin to these questions is the persistent mystery of evil and of suffering to which, in its normal reactions, Sunnī Islam often does less than justice. Reflection quickly makes it plain that suffering is tragically real in the house of Islam today, with its share in the pains and privations of "the third world," its pressures of population, its refugees, and, sharpest of all, the deep enmities and passions created by the insertion and expansion of the state of Israel. Islam instinctively replies to suffering with the doggedness of endurance. As Surah 47:35 directs: "Do not falter or sue for peace; you will be the upper ones"—a verse quoted in a sermon in the Great Mosque in Mecca just after the June war with Israel in 1967. Hardship and adversity are seen as trials and tribulations on the way to their reversal. They are not in themselves the fabric of redemptive victory. Mastery must be sought and found only in their manifest requital.

Here lie the deepest themes in the religious life of man. Islam believes in the evident, the effectual, the undeniable, the successful. Yet history does not always go that way. Injustice may be irreducible by outward means. Suffering is often the only right option left to truth. Perhaps the answer here is present already in the Islamic conviction of the Divine sovereignty, if this can be seen, beyond eschatology and judgment, as more ultimate than the enigmas of sin and evil through the greater strength of love and mercy.

There have been passionate sceptics in Islam despite the sanctions tending against their emergence or their toleration. The name of 'Umar al-Khayyām comes readily to mind. But of more radical intensity was the great blind poet Abū-l-'Alā' al-Ma'arrī, of Ma'arrat al-Nu'mān, a village in the Aleppo region of North Syria (973–1058 A.D.). Blind from the age of four because of smallpox, he became the most celebrated poet of his time and a legend after it. From beginnings as a panegyrist and a brief sojourn in intellectual circles in Baghdad, he returned to his native town on his mother's death, and developed a powerful criticism both of dogma and society, in poetry and letters, grim and unrelieved in their dark sense of tragedy, yet vividly human in their compassion. In his triple prison, "blindness, a narrow house, and a vile body," he considered all men blind where truth was at stake, preferring refuge in credulity or superstition, in dogma or authority. He wrote the most technically difficult verse in parable of the tedious strenuousness with which men engaged in life, artificial as it all was: *luzūm mā lam yalzam,* or "the necessity of the unnecessary," as it might be translated—a notion not far removed from contemporary ideas of "the absurd." We acquiesce in the pointless task of existing. His couplet on "The gates of birth" runs:

> Here am I laid, my father's infamy,
> But never any child accuses me.

Yet he was not all misanthropy. His letters to friends, in bereavement, at childbirth, in counsel, breathe a warm humanity and there was a wistfulness, akin to that of Thomas Hardy, about his incapacity to believe.

> Traditions have been handed down to me
> That would have had importance, would have had

But for my powers of credulity
Which are so bad.

Blindness and poetry are often allowed a liberty not readily available to the sighted and the prosaic. But the temper of Al-Maʿarrī and his kind, wherever it emerges, serves to keep the theism of Islam critical of its own confidence and, therefore, worthier in its ultimate quality. If we believe in God too readily, we surely believe in Him the less.

The years have gone like water, and they sweep
New populations to the shore of sleep.
The kingdoms are not swayed by man alone,
For God, in pity, dwells behind the throne.

But, with or without such chastening, what does the Islamic conviction mean in its final quality? What is it to "have" Allāh, to cry *Allāhu Akbar,* to live in the relevance of His prophets, His books, His religion and His judgment?

The answer must be as manifold as the house of Muslims. For the masses of ordinary believers it means a framework of belief and behavior, a preserving, demanding, encircling sense of God and duty. For the sophisticated it may mean only a habit of will, a cultural identity, a condition of life received from history. For the mystical it means "the shade of the wing of Gabriel," the abiding of the spirit under the remembrance of the Lord. To the activist it means the dynamism of a purposeful Heaven nurturing the ongoings of history. To the apostate in soul it is no more than the echo of a buried past. To the traditionalist it is a sacred trust to be served, with a steadfast fidelity both to the givenness of the Divine will and the hiddenness of the Divine knowledge. For the artists and builders, it is the inspirer of their forms, the indwelling of their domes, the cry from their minarets, the nurse of their skills.

Through all the diversities of its significance it is the invocation of the Name of the Merciful. "For all that is in the Qur'ān," declared Muḥammad, "is in the Opening Surah, and all that is in the Opening Surah is in the *Bismillah al-Raḥmān al-Raḥim:*" "In the Name of the merciful Lord of mercy."

Glossary

'abd: slave or servant—the status of man as doer of God's will, answering to *Rabb,* or "Lord," and linked with "worship," by the root verb.

adhān: the call to prayer made five times a day from every mosque.

'ajamī: foreign, i.e., non-Arabic, comparable to "barbarous" with the Greeks and to the original sense of "Wales" in English.

amānah: the trust of the earth given by God to man as having a delegated authority over nature.

amr: the word of command, the imperative by which the worlds came into being.

al-Amr bi-l-ma'rūf: the enjoining, in Islamic ethics, of what is right and sound and good, as conscience owns or knows it.

Asbāb al-Nuzūl: The "occasions of revelation." Situations or incidents with reference to which Muḥammad's deliverances under inspiration are to be understood; the context, not the cause, of the Qur'ān.

balāgh: the content of Muḥammad's preaching, as distinct from the sanctions or factors making for its acceptance or reacting to its rejection (see also *ḥisāb*).

Bismillāh: the phrase: "In the Name of the merciful Lord of Mercy," which prefaces every Surah save one (Surah 9); the general Islamic invocation of God.

Dār al-Islām: the house of Islam, the geographical realm and true domain of Muslim faith and practice; the territory in which Islam is in full devotional, political, and legal actuality.

Dār al-Ḥarb: the areas of mankind as yet unsubdued to Islam; the house of war, or struggle unto Islamization.

dhikr: the practice of recollection of God by mention of His Names reciprocally to God's reminder to men which is the Qur'ān. Among mystics *dhikr* is the technique, or discipline, of absorption in God.

dhimmī: a non-Muslim subject under Islamic rule, in one of the tolerated minorities: subject to special taxes in lieu of *Zakāt.*

Dīn: religion in general and religious duties in particular: incorporates the five basic obligations of the Muslim. The word also means Divine judgment.

Fātiḥah: title of the opening Surah of the Qur'ān, being "the Opener" of the Book.

fiqh: jurisprudence, the legal order of Islam as exercised in courts and expounded by the several Schools of Law.

fitnah: originally trial or persecution borne by believers in the Prophet: then sedition or conspiracy against the Islamic state; a basic concept relative to hostility and in its evolution a term reflecting the movement of early Islam from minority to majority status.

fuqahā': pl. of *faqīh,* jurisprudents, those learned in *fiqh* or applied law.

furqān: mainly a title of the Qur'ān, meaning the distinguisher or the criterion.

al-ghaib: the unseen, the realm of Divine mystery and ineffability.

Ḥadīth: Tradition in Islam from the standpoint of its reporting and recording, thus yielding Tradition as *Sunnah,* or obligatory law.

Ḥajj: pilgrimage to Mecca and its environs in the sacred month; the fifth Pillar of religion.

ḥanīf: a seeker after true religion, descriptive of Abraham in the Qur'ān as an anti-idolater; a God-fearer before Islam.

ḥifẓ al-Qur'ān: keeping (i.e., in heart reciting) the Qur'ān; memorizing as the due participation of the believer in the God-given words of Muḥammad.

Hijrah: the emigration of Muḥammad and his community from Mecca to Medina in 622 A.D., from which the Islamic calendar dates; the definitive crisis of Muḥammad's career.

ḥisāb: the business of reckoning with, or requiting, the rejection of preaching (*balāgh*); vindication of the message as distinct from its simple predication; the Divine "arithmetic" with men in time and eternity.

I'jāz: the quality of matchless eloquence attaching to the Qur'ān as revelation, whereby, for Islam, it constitutes a literary miracle; its style as evidence of its authenticity, Muḥammad being unlettered.

Ijmā': consensus, or converging, of approval; the means whereby the Muslim community in Sunnī Islam serves to identify loyal development in Islamic law and usage.

Ijtihād: the individual initiative of experts or pioneers whereby valid *Ijmā'* (previous term) is generated within the community, or (in Shī'ah Islam) is mediated to it.

Imām: the leader of mosque prayer: the spiritual Guide of Shī'ah Muslims by virtue of the "light of Muḥammad."

Imān: faith, the activity of belief, correlative to *Dīn,* or practice; supposed in, but sometimes distinguished from, *islām,* as submission or allegiance.

Islam: the faith, obedience and practice of Muḥammad's people, the final, perfected religion of God. Uncapitalized it denotes the quality of surrender to the Divine word and will which long antedates Islam.

isnād: the attestation of a tradition of Muḥammad through a chain of vouchers for its truth going back to his companions; what the tradition leans on, as distinct from what it says.

Jāhiliyyah: the time of ignorance in Arabia, preceding Islam, sometimes over-darkened; the ignorance involves an element of unruliness or uncouthness. Cf. the Biblical "froward."

Jihād: the concept of militancy on behalf of Islam to bring *Dār-al-Ḥarb* (q.v.)

into *Dār al-Islām;* also spiritualized as the mystic's struggle against evil within.

jizyah: the tax payable by *dhimmīs* (q.v.).

Kalām: lit. "speech." Denotes speculative theology in Islam.

Kalimah: the word or title given to the *Shahādah,* or confession: "There is no god but God; Muḥammad is the apostle of God."

kasb: acquisition: the view of a leading theologian, Al-Asha'rī, purporting to reconcile Divine disposition with human responsibility, through the formula: "God wills it *in* the will of the doer, who thus acquires the deed."

khilāfah: politically, the succession to the rule of Muḥammad from the first Caliph, Abu Bakr, down to 1924. ("Caliph" is the Anglicized form of *Khalīfah,* i.e., the possessor of *Khilāfah* or "caliphate.") Quranically the term means the status of Adam, or man, as trustee for God in the world.

kufr: antithetical to *shukr* (q.v.): the ultimate evil, disbelief in God and His signs, rejection of revelation, thanklessness.

ma'rūf: the well-doing Islam enjoins: things acknowledged as good.

matn: the substance of a tradition, as distinct from its *isnād* (q.v.) or support.

maulid: the Prophet's birthday, or a saint's birthday, celebrated with festive songs and gifts.

miḥrāb: the niche in the mosque which marks the *qiblah* (q.v.) of Mecca, the recess into which the *imām,* or prayer-leader, prays.

minbar: the mosque pulpit, often retractable, and at right angles to the *miḥrāb.*

muḥtasib: a superintendent, or inspector of ethical behavior; a spiritual accountant in the Muslim community.

mujtahid: one capable of, or exercising, *Ijtihād* (q.v.)

mu'jizah: the miracle of the Qur'ān, its quality as possessing *I'jāz* (q.v.).

mukhālafah: the difference, a technical term denoting the necessary distinction between a Name of God and the same adjective in human currency.

munkar: a thing vetoed or reproached, the ethically reprehensible.

muslim: one who believes in, belongs to, and performs *islām* (q.v.): the active participle of the verb to "islamize" or to "submit." (N.B. "Muhammadan" is never a proper descriptive. Muḥammad's people are "Muslims.")

mutawwi': lit. the "obediencer," an official in (e.g., Wahhābī) Islam whose business is to ensure moral and religious conformity.

Mu'tazilah: a group and school of theologians, strongest in the ninth century A.D., who pressed speculative matters about the Qur'ān and human free-will far beyond the position which later (and largely in reaction against them) came to be the orthodox dogma.

al-nabī al-ummī: the unlettered prophet. Muḥammad's role as the recipient of revelation without literary skill or personally gathered knowledge: or, the prophet to the Scriptureless.

al-Nahī 'an al-munkar: the prohibition of evil, false, and reprehensible behavior.

niyyah: intention, the conscious focus of purpose that must precede all ritual acts in Islam.

qadar: the Divine measure or determination of human events and actions; the decree, or power of God.

qiblah: the direction of prayer towards Mecca, by which every mosque is oriented and the house of Islam unified in *Ṣalāt* (q.v.).

qiyās: analogy, a provision whereby the law of Islam may be extended to cover situations analogous to, but not explicitly in, the Qur'ān and tradition.

Qur'ān: the recital, or reading: name of the sacred Scripture of Islam, believed communicated *verbatim* to Muḥammad and recited by him to his hearers and recorded, for their recitation, in 114 Surahs or chapters.

Rabb: Lord, the most frequent title of *Allāh,* often linked with ". . . of the worlds." See *'abd.*

Rasūl: messenger or apostle; the title of Muḥammad, though there are many *rusul,* (pl.) to a variety of peoples.

Rasūliyyah: the apostolate of Muḥammad, his dignity and duty both to proclaim and to vindicate the message from God.

ra'y: opinion or view (from the verb: to see) held or sponsored as a means to *Ijtihād* and *Ijmā'* (q.v.); a source, under conditions, of adaptation of law.

ṣadaqāt: voluntary alms, works of right-doing which show that faith is loyal.

Ṣalāt: ritual, or liturgical, prayer in Islam; the second Pillar of *Dīn,* performed five times daily.

Ṣaum: fasting, particularly during the month of Ramaḍan: the fourth Pillar of *Dīn;* lasts the whole lunar month during the daylight hours.

Shahādah: witness or confession, with intention, of the *Kalimah* (q.v.). The first Pillar of Islam.

Sharī'ah: the sacred law, grounded in the will of God, and given in the Qur'ān, tradition, *qiyās* and *Ijmā'* (q.v.): the path of duty, both ritual and general, for Muslims.

Shī'ah: the segment (lit. "sect") of Islam, in contradistinction to Sunnī Islam (q.v.), which originated in deep political, emotional and spiritual factors, in the first half century of Islam, and abides. Its themes of divergence are profound and elemental, relating to exegesis, eschatology, tradition, authority, and devotion.

Shirk: the cardinal sin of idolatry, or deification; any deviation from the sole worship of God; attribution of Divine power, knowledge, or will, to other than God.

shukr: gratitude or thankfulness, the proper human response to the Divine mercy; a favorite Quranic concern, contrasted with *kufr* (q.v.).

ṣūfī: the practicing mystic, often with ascetic attitudes. The term is derived from woollen (i.e., simple) dress characteristic of early Sufism. Sufis constitute a deep and vital element in Islamic life, history, and theology.

Sunnah: the path of tradition, the way of faith and conduct as followed by the (*Sunnī*) community of Islam.

Sunnī: the term denoting the broad mass of Islam from which the *Shī'ah* (q.v.) diverge. Sunnis reject the Shī'ah Imāms and rely on the Qur'ān, the Sunnah, and the community for the integrity and continuity of their Islam.

tafsīr: explanation, or exegesis, of the Qur'ān, involving Arabic grammar, study of *asbāb al-nuzūl* (q.v.) and erudition in tradition, allegory, abrogation, and commentary.

takbīr: the act of saying: *Allāhu Akbar*—"Great is God"; to magnify God.

taqlīd: hideboundness or authoritarianism in *tafsīr* (q.v.) of *fiqh* (q.v.); the state of adhering blindly to a traditional school; a frequent butt of modern reformers.

tarīqah: the Sufi way of discipline and initiation into Divine knowledge, through self-transcendence and self-mortification leading to the unitive state.

taslīm: the saying of "the peace of God be upon him," i.e., upon Muḥammad; the second half of the formula of benediction of the Prophet (see *taṣliyah*).

taṣliyah: the saying of "May God bless (lit. "pray upon") the Prophet" coupled always with *taslīm* (q.v.). This formula always follows mention of Muḥammad's name in orthodox speaking and writing.

tauḥīd: the assertion, or doctrine, of the Divine unity. God is One; let God be God alone; the driving motive and end of Islam.

ta'wīdh: the act of saying: "I seek refuge with God"—a frequent Quranic formula and one of the deepest themes of Islamic devotion.

'ulamā': (pl. of *'ālim*) doctors of theology or law, learned ones, the custodians of Islamic teachings.

Ummah: a very inclusive term—the community of Islam, the solidarity of faith and prayer, the political incorporation of the faith, the people of the allegiance.

ummī: unlettered, one of a people without Scriptures, or illiterate. See *al-nabī al-ummī.*

'urf: customary law, brought into Islam from the conquered peoples on condition of its compatibility with Islamic sources.

waḥy: the recipience of revelation by Muḥammad; the state of receptivity in which he received and communicated the Qur'ān; revelation and inspiration are not here distinguished.

Zakāt: almsgiving, the third Pillar of *Dīn;* property and possessions obligate men to society: what we pay validates what we own.

ẓulm: wrong-doing, or wrong dealing, the most fundamental Quranic term for sin.

Notes

Introduction

[1] Translated from Jamāl 'Abd al-Nāṣir, *Falsafat al-Thaurah,* Cairo, 1953. An edition in English was published in Washington, D.C., by Public Affairs Press, in 1955, with the title: *Egypt's Liberation: The Philosophy of the Revolution.*

Chapter 1

[1] To add "submission" and "submitter" after the Arabic terms "Islam" and "Muslim" might be useful. But it would also distort, and possibly prejudice, the whole meaning which has to develop through an entire book. "Islam" of course is the thing done and "Muslim" is the doer of it. The root contains the vital consonants: S-L-M and relates to "surrender," "peace," "safety," "salutation," "resignation," and "immunity." It would be sad to curtail so full a concept by a premature simplicity. In general, Arabic terms will be found elucidated in the immediate context of their first use. There is also the Glossary.

[2] *Kitāb al-Luma'* (The Book of Insight), translated by R. J. McCarthy, Beirut, 1953, p. 56.

[3] *Ibid.,* pp. 99–100.

[4] Duncan B. Macdonald, *Development of Muslim Theology, Jurisprudence and Constitutional Theory,* New York, 1903, pp. 314–15.

[5] *Ibid.,* p. 303.

[6] *Ibid.,* pp. 303–04.

[7] *Ibid.,* pp. 304–08.

Chapter 2

[1] The early and deep schism among Muslims which gave rise to Shī'ah Islam will be explored in Chapter 6. The dominant and successful majority came to be known as "Sunnis," holding to the emerging political and legal "orthodoxy" of Islam against these unsuccessful schismatics—the "deviationists" or "sectarians."

Chapter 3

[1] Western orientalism has done much to foster the counterpart of an "Islamic orientalism." The former is seen by the latter as, in part, a worthy scholarship Muslims can emulate and, in part, the stranger's distortions or misinterpretations which Muslims must rectify. Quranic translation and study are the first of these fields. The leaders of the Aḥmadiyyah Movements, for example, in the twentieth century, set themselves to give their own translations of the Qur'ān in the western languages.

[2] Arberry's fullest discussion of the issues in translation is found in his *The Holy Koran,* London, 1953, being selections appearing in advance of the complete edition.

[3] A. J. Arberry, *The Koran Interpreted,* New York, 1956. Surah 94.

[4] N. J. Dawood, *The Koran,* Baltimore, 2nd revised edition, 1966, p. 26. This translator follows his own chronological arrangement and uses no verse numberings.

[5] Translations from the Qur'ān in this work, save for the two noted in the two preceding footnotes, are by the author.

Chapter 4

[1] See F. W. Nietzsche, *The Birth of Tragedy,* translated by F. Golffing, New York, 1956, p. 11.

[2] The canonical sources of the Sharī'ah are involved in the tensions belonging with the Sunnī/Shī'ah controversies, noted in their historical setting in Chapter 6.

[3] John Williams, *Islam,* New York, 1960, p. 96.

Chapter 5

[1] There are innumerable Arabic prayer manuals, containing such personal devotions for various occasions, intimate or mundane. Their more theological implications are studied in C. E. Padwick, *Muslim Devotions,* London, 1961. The Aḥmadiyyah in Islam published an English prayer book in 1955, at Lahore, with the title: *A Muslim Prayer Book.*

[2] Political unrest and theological questioning found sharp expression by the Kharijites (or *Khawārij*), a militant movement, based mainly on Basrah, from the middle of the seventh century A.D. Denouncing the excesses of the Umayyads, the Kharijites held that they were not true Muslims, since their "works" did not corroborate their profession of "faith." Not being valid Muslims they had no right to rule: allegiance to them must be withdrawn. The question of "faith" and "works" in turn excited the problem of human and Divine will. How was it that men could go counter to the Divine law?

[3] Quoted from W. Montgomery Watt's translation of *Al-Munqidh min al-Ḍalāl,* in *The Faith and Practice of Al-Ghazali,* London, George Allen & Unwin Ltd., 1953, pp. 54, 56, and 58.

[4] "The accursed (lit. "the stoned") Satan" (*al Shaiṭān al-Rajīm*), is a recurrent Quranic phrase and may be understood in a sense close to the Biblical idea of "the accuser," the *diabolos,* who defies God in contesting the very creation of man, the creature, and his gift of the dominion over nature (see Surah 2:30 f.).

Chapter 6

[1] The relation between the Islamic and the Christian calendars can be readily seen from the table of parallel important dates preceding the text. A complete table for the conversion of Muslim/Christian dates from the Hijrah to the year 2000 A.D. is given in G. S. P. Freeman-Grenville, *The Muslim and Christian Calendars,* London, 1963.

[2] They may be seen in the introverted, insulated attitudes traditional until the twentieth century among Christian and Jewish groups in the Middle East, and in the legal tangle of community personal law which is only lately being "rationalized." Lebanon is the clearest example of the communal religious allegiances within a common citizenship.

Chapter 7

[1] Published by René Guillard, Paris, 1962.

[2] See *The Autobiography of Malcolm X,* New York, 1964, pp. 338–347.

[3] Franz Rosenthal, *The Muqaddimah: an Introduction to History,* translated from the Arabic, 3 vols., New York, 1958.

[4] *Ibid.* See Vol. 2, p. 436 and Vol. 3, pp. 36–38. The author sharply separates philosophy from theology and sees the former, at best, of value only to certain individuals, and defensively in relation to faith. Cf. Vol. 3, pp. 52–55.

Bibliography

An invaluable tool for pursuing bibliographical questions in Islamic studies is: J. D. Pearson: *Index Islamicus, 1906–1955,* published at Cambridge, in 1958, and the same compiler's *Index Islamicus: Supplement, 1956–1960,* Cambridge, 1962.

Though the titles suggested below are arranged in line with the chapters of *The House of Islam,* many relate to all, or most, of the themes of this book.

1. Lord of the Worlds

Encyclopedia of Islam, 1913–1938, Leiden, Holland, and the Revised edition, begun in 1954. See article on Allah.

H. A. R. Gibb: *Muhammadanism: a Historical Survey,* revised edition, 1961, New York. A lucid and effective introductory presentation, with a useful book list.

K. W. Morgan, ed.: *Islam, the Straight Path,* New York, 1958. A collection of essays in confession of Islam by a number of Asian writers, and exposition from within.

Fazlur Rahman: *Islam,* London, 1961. Another work of thorough and competent scholarship from within Islam.

Alfred Guillaume: *Islam,* London, 1954. D. Sourdel: *Islam,* New York, 1962 (translated from French). John A. Williams: *Islam,* London, 1961. Three short, general surveys, presenting basic material. Williams annotates extracts from Muslim sources and there are several useful insights in Guillaume, coming from a long erudition which he does not obtrude.

W. Montgomery Watt: *Islamic Philosophy and Theology* (Islamic Surveys, No. 1), Edinburgh, 1962. A brief and sharply condensed summary of the main themes, schools, and figures, in classic Muslim thought about God, arranged in historical sequence, with very full bibliography.

A. J. Wensinck: *The Muslim Creed,* Cambridge, 1932. Daud Rahbar: *God of Justice: A Study of Ethical Doctrine of the Qur'an,* Leiden, 1960. Two exacting but representative works on Muslim theology. Rahbar breaks new ground in his exhaustive treatment of Quranic contexts in elucidating its teaching about Divine will and being.

Duncan B. Macdonald: *Development of Muslim Theology, Jurisprudence and Constitutional Theory,* New York, 1903. An older work, still to be consulted with profit.

2. Muḥammad and the Rasūliyyah

Tor Andrae: *Muhammad, the Man and his Faith,* translated from the German, by T. Menzel, New York, 1960. Much the most vivid and adequate presentation of the genesis of the Prophet's mission and the psychology of his vocation in the pre-Hijrah period.

Arthur Jeffery: *Islam, Muhammad and his Religion,* New York, 1958. An anthology from Muslim sources, covering all the main elements in the religious life of Islam, with a valuable glossary and a very large number of Quranic citations.

W. Montgomery Watt: *Muhammad, Prophet and Statesman,* London, 1961. The best single introduction to the biographical study of Muḥammad, condensing the same author's two larger works on Muḥammad in Mecca and in Medina. A work of careful scholarship.

Muhammad Ali: *The Living Thoughts of Muhammad,* London, 1950. Abd al-Rahman Azzam: *The Eternal Message of Muhammad,* translated by C. E. Farah New York, 1964. Two popular Muslim presentations of the meaning and significance of the founder of Islam, in modern terms.

Richard Bell: *Origin of Islam in its Christian Environment,* London, 1926. C. C. Torrey: *Jewish Foundation of Islam,* Yale, 1933. Two works by outstanding scholars, the one giving the case for a general Christian, the other for a largely Jewish, indebtedness of original Islam. Attempts to document the bearing of "the people of the Book" on the antecedents of Muḥammad.

A. Guillaume, trans.: *Life of Muhammad,* Oxford, 1955. An English rendering of Ibn Isḥāq's *Sīrat Rasūl Allāh,* one of the earliest full length biographies of the Prophet. Invaluable for the atmosphere and authentic savor of what happened in the Qur'ān.

———: *The Traditions of Islam,* London, 1954. A useful introduction to the vast field of traditions, with some account of their development and examples.

3. Qur'ān

A. J. Arberry: *The Koran Interpreted,* New York, 1956. Much the best English rendering of the Islamic Scripture, striving to match the meter and temper of the original Arabic. (This is what is referred to in the word "Interpreted" in the title which, otherwise, would be misleading. This is not a commentary.)

———: *The Holy Koran, an Introduction with Selections,* London, 1953. The translation is the same as the above, but this group of special passages is prefaced, as the full work is not, with a detailed analysis of the problems of Arabic/English translation and of how the translator has handled them.

N. A. Dawood: *The Koran,* New York, 1960. Another very useful translation, in places even more intelligible than Arberry's. The drawback here is that the translator rearranges the Qur'ān chronologically. But, in this laudable venture, he gives no explanations or clues to his decisions, and the book is awkward to use, for lack of this and for lack of verse numberings. Every passage has to be tracked down laboriously, though by this means the user does get to know the Qur'ān.

Richard Bell: *Introduction to the Qur'ān,* Edinburgh, 1963. All that the general student needs is here, about the technical problems and issues of Quranic study. This is an indispensable tool.

W. Montgomery Watt: *Companion to the Qur'ān,* Edinburgh, 1968. A companion of somewhat economical conversation, who does, however, offer brief, illuminating comments and observations on every chapter, with useful wayside notes.

4. Law

N. J. Coulson: *A History of Islamic Law,* Edinburgh, 1964. (Islamic Surveys, No. 2). Joseph Schacht: *Introduction to Islamic Law,* Oxford, 1964. Two competent manuals.

A. Jeffery: *A Reader on Islam,* 'S Gravenhage, 1962. An ample anthology of "Passages from standard Arabic writings illustrative of the beliefs and practices of Muslims." An invaluable source book of religious life, the gathering and editing of which presents a lifetime of devoted Islamic scholarship.

Reuben Levy: *The Social Structure of Islam,* London, 1957. A revised edition of the author's *Sociology of Islam* (1933), with chapters on the status of women, of children, and of the Caliphate, in Islam, and moral sentiments and social customs among Muslims.

Abdul-Hakim Khalifa: *Islamic Ideology,* Lahore, 1951. M. R. Sharif: *Islamic Social Framework,* Lahore, 1954. Two representative Pakistani expositions of the themes of law, society, state and ethics, in Islam.

R. Roberts: *Social Laws of the Qur'ān,* London, 1925. An older, but serviceable, short presentation of the subject.

D. M. Donaldson: *Muslim Ethics,* London, 1953. May be consulted on particular themes, though some of its judgments are debatable.

I. Izutsu: *Ethical Doctrine of the Qur'ān,* Montreal, 1967. Through contextual study of certain basic moral terms and concepts in the Qur'ān, the Japanese scholar offers an original discussion of the mores of Islam.

T. Arnold and A. Guillaume, eds.: *The Legacy of Islam,* London 1931. A delightful volume with a variety of contributors and topics. Note especially Guillaume himself on Theology, and David de Santillana on Law and Society.

5. Liturgy

H. Lammens: *Islam, Beliefs and Practices,* translated from French by E. Denison Ross, London, 1929. A scholarly exposition.

G. E. von Grunebaum: *Muhammadan Festivals,* New York, 1951. Presents from several larger, authoritative works, the rudiments of Muslim works of *Dīn,* or religion.

Ahmad Kamal: *The Sacred Journey,* New York, 1961. A popular, reverent manual of the pilgrimage rites with translations of prayers, and interpretation of participation.

Constance E. Padwick: *Muslim Devotions,* London, 1961. A careful, sensitive, and highly competent presentation of the major themes, phrases, attitudes and emphases of Islamic personal religion, drawn from a lifelong study of pocket manuals of prayer and praise, gathered through much loving converse with their users in markets and mosques across the Muslim world. A veritable treasure.

A. J. Arberry: *Sufism,* London, 1950. An introduction to a vast and exacting field of study.

6. Ummah

A. J. Arberry, ed.: *Aspects of Islamic Civilization,* Ann Arbor, 1967. A rich stimulus to the imagination and a comprehensive, expertly chosen, canvas of Islamic life, translated from original sources, Arabic and Persian.

R. Roolvink, et al.: *Historical Atlas of the Islamic Peoples,* Cambridge, Mass., 1957. Traces in competent color maps and charts the sequence of Islamic Caliphates and the territorial expression of Islam through fourteen centuries.

Carl Brockelmann: *History of the Islamic Peoples,* London, 1947. From the German original. The handiest and most utilized one-volume history of Islam.

Bernard Lewis: *The Middle East and the West,* New York, 1964. A useful, recent survey of the bearings of Arab Islam in the last two and a half centuries.

Sayyid Hosein Nasr: *Ideals and Realities of Islam,* London, 1967. A presentation of Islamic ethos from the standpoint of an alert and articulate Shīʿah Muslim of Persian nationality.

7. *Questions of Time*

W. C. Smith: *Islam in Modern History,* Princeton, 1957. Careful and penetrating reflection on the modern destiny and evolution of Islam, in the Arab, Pakistanī, Indian, Turkish and African scene. A work of significance in intercultural interpretation.

E. I. J. Rosenthal: *Islam in the Modern Nation State,* Cambridge, 1965. Studies the contemporary expression of Islamic ideas and forms in terms of twentieth century nationalism.

A. J. Arberry, general ed.: *Religion in the Middle East: Concord and Conflict,* Cambridge, 1968, 2 vols. Volume 1 contains a comprehensive account of the Islamic aspects, under the subeditorship of C. F. Beckingham. An important major work.

J. H. Thompson and R. D. Reischauer, eds.: *Modernization in the Arab World,* Princeton, 1966. A symposium on the economic, political and social aspects of modernity and a useful measure of the current setting of religious obligation and challenge.

H. A. R. Gibb: *Modern Trends in Islam,* Chicago, 1946. Twenty years old and, therefore, factually in arrears, but still a penetrating analysis of the issues involved for Muslim faith and order in the new dimensions of the twentieth century.

G. S. Métraux and F. Crouzet, eds.: *The New Asia,* New York, 1965. A series of papers written in association with U.N.E.S.C.O. and *The Journal of World History.* Assesses Islam in Turkey and the Arab world.

A. A. A. Fyzee: *A Modern Approach to Islam,* Bombay, 1963. A short, but illuminating, example of the ventures of Islamic loyalty in reinterpretation and rapport with other faiths, in this case mainly with Hinduism.

Ibn Khaldūn: *The Muqaddimah,* translated by F. Rosenthal and abridged by N. A. Dawood, London, 1967. Brings the great classic of history within the reach of English readers.

Kenneth Cragg: *Counsels in Contemporary Islam,* Edinburgh, 1965 (Islamic Surveys, No.3). Offers a very full bibliography of modern Muslim writing and a review of the major themes and movements of its inner debate.

———: *The Call of the Minaret,* New York, 1956. The middle section is entitled: "Minaret and Muslim."

———: *The Dome and the Rock,* London, 1964, and *The Privilege of Man,* London, 1968. Some account of the shape of religious life in Islam and a study of the Islamic concept of man the "caliph" of God and its relevance to our contemporary triumphs and dilemmas. See Preface.

Index

Theodicy, 16f
Theology in Islam, 8f; fatalism and, 12; scholastic, 12f
Theonomy, 17
Time, 12
Al-Tirmīdhī, 27
Toleration in Islam, 81f, 85, 88
Torah, 7, 38, 45
Tradition, 24, 26f, 47, 49, 51, 53, 60, 80, 98; in exegesis, 40; *isnād* of, 26, 101; *matn* of, 26, 102
Tragedy in human situation, 15f, 98
Transcendence, in Islam, 13f, 45, 56
Translation, of the Qur'ān, 31f; exegesis in, 34
Tribalism, 21, 72
Tripolitania, 74
Tunisia, 55, 68, 74, 77, 82, 90, 91, 95
Turkey, 2, 55, 82, 95 97
Turkism, 2
Turks, 31, 77, 88, 92
Twelvers, the, 79f

Uḥud, Battle of, 22
'Ulamā', 50, 76, 95, 104
'Umar, 25, 74, 75
Umayyads, 64, 74, 76, 77, 80
Ummah, 4, 25, 27, 50, 59, 70, 72f, 104
'Umrah, 70
Unitarianism, problem of, 16, 92, 93
Universality, of Islam, 86f, 94
Urbanization, 3
'urf, 51, 104
'Uthmān, 38, 74, 76, 78

Vocabulary, 7, 33, 40

Wahhabism, 87, 91f
Waḥy, 26, 35, 38, 104
Wālī Ullāh, Shah, 93
West, the, 83, 84, 88, 93
Will, of God, 7, 13f
Wonder, religious, 15f
Worship, 6, 7, 56, 57; false, 11, imagination in, 15
wuḍū', 58

Yahweh, 6
Yathrib, 20

Zabūr, 38
Zain al-'Ābidīn, 79
Zakāt, 47f, 56, 67, 104
Zamzam, well of, 70
Zionism, 2
Ẓulm, 11, 16, 104

Quranic Quotations

Surah	1	59
	2:1	97
	2:23	35
	2:153	61
	2:170	72
	2:183 to 187	67
	2:191	21
	2:196 to 197	69
	2:255	29
Surah	3:7	40
	3:83	11
	3:97	69
Surah	4:3	54
	4:34	55
	4:157	34
Surah	5:60	28
	5:104	72
Surah	6:12	16
Surah	7:180	10
	7:206	61
Surah	8:45	28
Surah	9:75	28
	9:103	48
Surah	10:38	35
	10:78	72
Surah	11:12	35
Surah	13:12	13
	13:18	13
	13:28	62
	13:40	21
Surah	17:2	28, 63
	17:22 to 39	52
	17:106	35
Surah	18:83	37
Surah	21:16	57
Surah	22:24	37
Surah	24:35 to 37	39
	24:40	28
	24:53	21
Surah	25	43, 44
	25:32	35
Surah	29:17	21
Surah	30:1	37
	30:21	54
Surah	31:13	11
Surah	33:22	28
	33:33	81
	33:42	61
	33:56	29
	33:57	29
Surah	36:16	21
Surah	41:44	31
Surah	42:47	21
Surah	43:3	32
Surah	44:38	57
Surah	47:35	98
Surah	72:24	28